The Essex

in
Circular Walks

Paul Bentley

Jacqui Farrants

Half Way Publishing

Kelvedon, Essex

First published August 2020

Copyright: Jacqui Farrants and Paul Bentley

All rights reserved. No reproduction permitted without prior permission of the publishers.

Published by:

Half Way Publishing

Printed by:

Lavenham Press Ltd

ISBN:

978-1-5272-6624-7

Photographs by Paul Bentley

Maps by Trevor Johnson

Front and back cover design by Lavenham Press Ltd

Contents

Disclaimer   5

Introduction   6

About the Book   7

About the Walks   9

Abbreviations   11

Map of The Essex Way   12

The Walks

1. Epping to Colliers Hatch	7 miles	15
2. Colliers Hatch to Greensted	6.5 miles	20
3. Greensted to Witney Green	8 miles	25
4. Witney Green to Peppers Green	7.5 miles	31
5. Peppers Green to Round Roblets	6.5 miles	36
6. Round Roblets to Pleshey	7.5 miles	41
7. Pleshey to Chatham Green	8 miles	46
8. Chatham Green to Fuller Street	6 miles	51
9. Fuller Street to Fairstead	4.5 miles	56
10. Fairstead to White Notley	6 miles	61
11. White Notley to Bradwell	7.5 miles	66
12. Bradwell to Coggeshall	8.5 miles	71
13. Coggeshall to Great Tey	6.5 miles	78

14. Great Tey to Fordham	7.5 miles	83
15. Fordham to Great Horkesley	7.5 miles	88
16. Great Horkesley to Boxted	8.5 miles	93
17. Boxted to Stratford St Mary	8.5 miles	98
18. Stratford St Mary to Lawford	8 miles	103
19. Lawford to Mistley	6.5 miles	108
20. Mistley to Wrabness	8 miles	113
21. Wrabness to Ramsey	6.5 miles	118
22. Ramsey to Dovercourt	6 miles	124
23. Dovercourt to Harwich	6 miles	128

Further Reading   133

Disclaimer

At the time of publication all walks followed public rights of way or permissive paths, and great care has been taken to ensure accuracy of the directions, however details can change. In particular, there are quite a few new housing developments appearing throughout the region at this time, which may result in some rerouting of footpaths. The authors cannot accept responsibility for any inaccuracies in the book that may result from such changes. It is suggested that you take with you the relevant Ordnance Survey map and always walk with safety, consideration and respect for property.

THE ESSEX WAY IN CIRCULAR WALKS

Introduction

The Essex Way is a long-distance waymarked footpath, stretching 81 miles from Epping in the southwest of the county to Harwich in the northeast. It is the result of a competition in 1972 by the Essex branch of the Council of the Protection of Rural England, linking ancient green lanes and footpaths.

The route passes through areas of outstanding natural beauty and is an absolute joy to walk, as it takes in all the best of the countryside the county has to offer. There are striking variations in the terrain along the way, from the dense and ancient forests of Epping, to the undulating Dedham Vale that inspired painter John Constable, opening out on to the breezy Stour Estuary and the seaside at Harwich.

The route is waymarked by Essex County Council plaques, sporting two red poppies, although the eagle-eyed may spot some of the very few remaining original dark green markers along the way.

About the Book

As with all long-distance linear routes, the Essex Way presents the dilemma of how best to tackle it. One option is to walk the length of it in one go, stopping overnight at hostelries en route. However, this requires some planning and sufficient stamina to carry any luggage required. Furthermore, alas, there are many fewer pubs offering accommodation in Essex than there once were.

One alternative is to divide the route into sections and walk one stretch at a time at one's convenience. This has the advantage of not requiring overnight stopover points but has the drawback of having to get back to each start point. While this can be solved in some places by using public transport, bus and rail services are scarcer these days, leaving some stretches of the Essex Way poorly served.

Another option is to take two cars and park one at each end of the route, in what we like to call the two-car-tango. But this is less than ideal as it means travelling separately from your companion, doesn't work for the lone traveller and isn't great for the environment. And so that leaves the option of retracing your steps back along the same route to the start, which can feel repetitive.

This book is our solution to the problem. We made each route into a circular walk, enabling us to return to each start point on foot. The first part of each walk takes you from a convenient parking spot to a point on the Essex Way then, after a few miles on the Essex Way, the route takes you back to the start.

Each walk picks up at the point on the Essex Way where the previous one left off so, by following all the walks in the book, you will have covered the whole of the Essex Way, plus some equally lovely countryside that doesn't normally get the same attention.

Detailed directions have been provided for all parts of the route. Although the Essex Way is clearly marked for most of the way, signage can be patchy in places. We found that some other Essex

Way walking guides don't always include sufficiently detailed instructions and cover routes that may be too long for the casual walker. So, with thorough directions that are easy to follow, and lengths to suit both the afternoon rambler as well as the long-distance hiker, we hope you will find this book a reliable companion on your journey for the whole 81 miles however you choose to walk it.

About the Walks

The twenty-three walks in this book range in length from 4½ to 8½ miles and each includes three or more miles of the Essex Way. All distances are approximate and rounded to the nearest half mile, and all routes are circular. They can be walked in any order or combined to form longer walks.

The title of each walk represents the section of the Essex Way that's covered, not the start of the walk itself, which is usually a parking spot at a nearby village, for which an address and postcode is provided. Any pubs along the route are also noted.

Only public access routes are included, such as footpaths, bridleways, lanes and other tracks. We have tried, where possible to find the shortest, most direct route to and from the Essex Way while avoiding main roads and ensuring a pleasant walk all round. This means that, in a few cases, the route may criss-cross or repeat a brief section of Essex Way.

The walks are largely dog-friendly, although you may need a lead for the occasional road or area of livestock. Most footpaths are clearly marked although, inevitably, some signage may be incomplete in places. It's also worth noting that the terrain may change at different times of the year. For example, field footpaths that are very visible when the summer crops are high, may be less obvious in the winter months.

We have done our best to guide the walker using other landmarks, as well as providing the corresponding OS map number for each walk for additional reference. You can also get an OS map app for your smart phone which we found particularly useful. You'll need to subscribe to the Leisure Map option for full footpath coverage. The advantage of an app over a paper map is that it can pinpoint exactly where you are, not just where you think you should be, and reduces the need for heated debate! We have included outline maps, marking the Essex Way section of the routes in red. In the directions, the joining and leaving points of the Essex Way sections are noted in bold for those wanting to combine walks to make longer stretches. For further navigation, please note the abbreviations used in this book.

Abbreviations

L	Left
R	Right
TL	Turn Left
TR	Turn Right
SA	Straight Ahead
FP	Footpath/Bridleway
FPS	Footpath Sign (includes fingerposts, waymark posts and bridleways)
LHFE	Left Hand Field Edge
RHFE	Right Hand Field Edge
EW	Essex Way

THE ESSEX WAY IN CIRCULAR WALKS

The Essex Wa

THE ESSEX WAY IN CIRCULAR WALKS

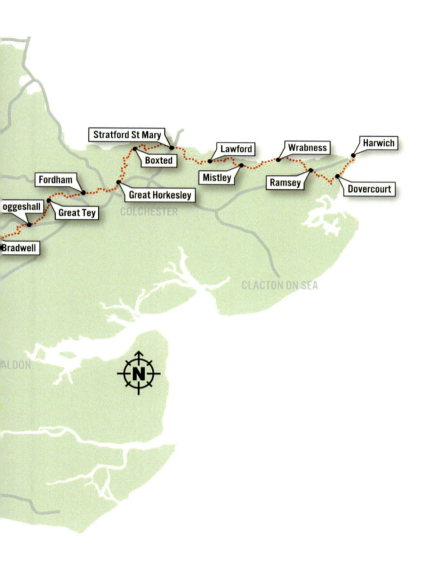

The Walks

THE ESSEX WAY IN CIRCULAR WALKS

1: Epping to Colliers Hatch

Total distance: 7 miles

Of which Essex Way: 3.5 miles

Map: OS Explorer 174 & 183 (TL 500 013)

Parking: The walk starts at what is no longer, alas, The Mole Trap pub, Tawney Common, Epping CM16 7PU. You can park, with consideration, on the street.

Pubs on route: The Merry Fiddlers, Fiddlers Hamlet; The Theydon Oak, Coopersale Street.

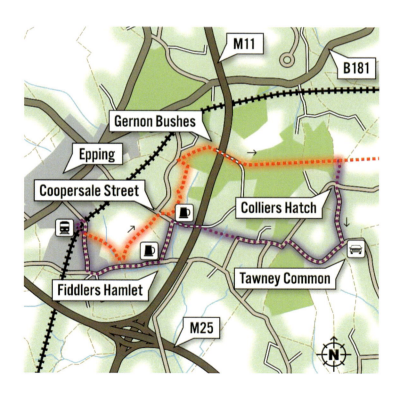

Walk Overview

This opening walk in the book covers the first section of the Essex Way from its start at Epping underground station. The walk begins at Tawney Common and heads towards Epping where it picks up the start of the Essex Way to take us through a peaceful nature reserve for a pleasant woodland stroll before heading back to Tawney Common.

Directions

1) With the pub behind you, TL to walk to the T-junction and take the lane to the R signposted Theydon Mount and Epping. Follow the road as it bends round past Tawney Farm on the L and continue on this lane for around half a mile, passing the woods on the L until you reach a Y-junction. TL toward Theydon Mount and Epping.

2) Continue on this road for around half a mile, passing the road to Theydon Mount on the L and, as the road bends to the L at Gaynes Park, take the FP ahead to the R toward Coopersale Street. Follow the RHFE with views across the countryside to the L and continue SA through the gap in the hedge into the next field, keeping to the RHFE.

3) At the end of the field, on reaching the fence just before the motorway, TR for a few yards, then TL to cross the bridge over the motorway. Take the FP to the L for a few yards and then TR to keep to the RHFE heading downhill. At the end of the field, cross the stream and continue, with the fence to the L and the hedge to the R, then go through a gate to reach the road. TL onto the road and pass the house on the L calling itself Great Oak, although it looks more like an old school, and into Fiddlers Hamlet, passing the Victorian post-box in the wall to the R, to reach the T-junction.

4) TR toward Epping and Ivy Chimneys, passing The Merry Fiddlers on the L. Continue SA, eventually passing the golf course on your L and ignoring (for now) the EW signs to the R (as we're headed to the start of the EW first). Pass Stewards Green and Stewards Close on the R and follow the main road as it bends round to the R onto Bower Hill toward Epping Town Centre. Almost at the top of the hill, opposite Bower Vale on the L, you will see an EW FP to the R. At this point, if you wish, you can start the EW section of the walk – skip Directions 5 and 6 and go straight to Direction 7.

5) Or, if you're a purist, you can continue for a few hundred yards to the very start of the EW at Epping Station. To do this, after a few yards, TL to walk up Hillcrest Way, cross the bridge over the railway tracks and TL to walk along the pavement to the front of the station and the plaque that marks the start of the EW.

6) We now start on the EW section of the walk. Retrace your steps, back over the railway and down Hillcrest Way, and then TR onto the road, then cross the road to take the FP to the L. (Note the concrete EW sign here, unusually bearing the inscription *Essex Way* instead of the usual "Public Footpath" lettering).

7) Follow the path along the back of the houses, then between fields, through the gap in the hedge on the R, and TL to continue on the LHFE until you reach the road. At this point you should be feeling a sense of déjà vu. TL for a few yards, then take the next FP to the L at another concrete sign that also bears the *Essex Way* inscription. Follow the EW signs through the trees (sections of this can be muddy in winter). On reaching the road, TR toward Fiddlers Hamlet and Toot Hill, walking past the Theydon Oak on the L. On the bend and just before South Lodge, take the partially obscured FP to the L. (If you get as far as Gaynes Park, you've missed it).

8) On reaching a gate, follow the signs round the LHFE and, at the end of the field, go diagonally L across the next field. Once across the field TR to keep on the LHFE, then continue along the next field, on the LHFE to head toward the woods. Follow the path into the Nature Reserve, and then TL, following the signs along this shady woodland walk. (This area is known as Gernon Bushes, a site of special scientific interest; an ancient coppice with pollarded hornbeams, areas of marsh with rare plants and ponds created following gravel quarrying). Continue round past the information board, then past the school on the L. Exit the woods via the wooden kissing gate and continue SA, following the fence-line to the R, keeping to the R of the sports field, then back into the Nature Reserve and TL through the forest and over the motorway, then back into the woods on the other side. Continue for a long straight walk all the way through the forest, ignoring any other crossing paths. (On a tree marked with a white arrow, we found a very old and unusual six-sided EW sign. On reaching the edge of the forest and junction of FPs, **we now leave the EW**.

9) Take the FP to the R to reach the road. TL for a few yards, then TR up Tawney Common and follow this quiet country lane to return to the pub.

Start of the Essex Way at Epping

Lunchtime

Tree-lined path

THE ESSEX WAY IN CIRCULAR WALKS

2: Colliers Hatch to Greensted

Total distance: **6.5** miles

Of which Essex Way: 3.5 miles

Map: OS Explorer 174 & 183 (TL 538 028)

Parking: The walk starts at the car park of St Andrew's Church, Church Lane, Greensted, CM5 9LD.

Pubs on route: The Green Man, School Road, Toot Hill.

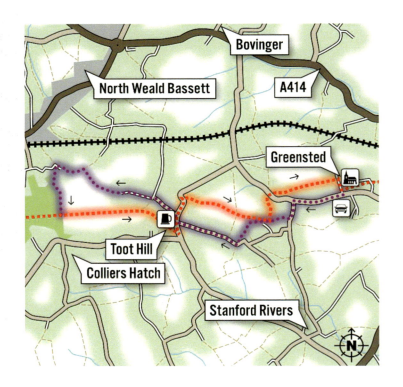

Walk Overview

The walk begins at Greensted and takes us through quiet country lanes and open fields to Toot Hill. Then, after a stroll through the forest, we join the Essex Way near Colliers Hatch for a cross-country route back to Greensted and the oldest wooden church in the world.

Directions

1) Walk away from the church toward the end of Church Lane and TR onto the main road. After around a quarter of a mile TL, passing Hillside House on the R. Just after Repentance Cottage take the FP to the R to walk along the RHFE. Toward the end of the field and the junction of FPs, ignore the wooden kissing gate on the R and continue SA to join the EW for around 50 yds. At a metal gate on the L, leave the EW to take the FP diagonally L through the trees.

2) Exit the forest via a metal gate, then ignore the FP to the R and head across the field, slightly diagonally L. Ignore the next FP to the L, then continue on the LHFE toward Toot Hill. On reaching the road TR. After around 200yds, on reaching some houses, notice the old George VI post-box that's been painted black and placed in the wall of Granville House to the L.

3) At the T-junction at the end of Toot Hill Road TR toward Greensted, Bobbingworth and Ongar. After a few yards, TL onto Mill Lane, ignoring the FP to the L just after the equestrian centre. At the end of the lane, at the water tower, ignore the FP to the R and continue SA onto a dirt track, and onto the public bridleway toward North Weald. Keep to the L at the derelict barn to take a covered bridleway through the trees. Stay on this long leafy path, eventually passing a fishing lake on the R. At the end of the woods, the site of the old Roman road runs across your path from L to R, although it's barely visible now.

4) Exit the forest and TR to walk along the RHFE. At the end of the field and the signage, TL to walk along the LHFE. At the field corner TR, keeping the wall of Cold Hall Farm to the L, and follow it round, still keeping to the LHFE. Across the field to the R, you can see part of the old Epping Ongar railway that is now a heritage line running steam trains between Ongar and North Weald. (For further information and some interesting walks, we thoroughly recommend David Gridley's excellent *Walking the Lost Railways of Essex*). At the junction of bridleway signs, TL and cross the lane to take the FP signposted Bassett Millennium Walks, heading toward the forest on a broad grassy track. On reaching the forest TL at the waymark to walk along the RHFE with the forest on your R, until you reach a wooden vertical, four-way signpost.

5) TL to join the EW. Keep to the LHFE and continue on this long straight path between fields for about half a mile, which includes a surprisingly steep uphill section. TR through the hedge and then diagonally L across the field. At the end of the field continue through to the next field keeping to the LHFE. Follow the EW signs through a covered pathway and over a stile to a rough meadow, round the side of a paddock and over a stile to the road.

6) TL onto the road, passing the Green Man pub. Experience a brief sense of déjà vu as we cover our earlier tracks for a few yards. Pass Mill Lane on the L then, after around 150yds, as the road bends to the L, take the FP to the R at Weald Lodge. TR to follow the RHFE for a few yards, then TR over a plank bridge, just past "The Cottage" (!). Follow this pretty covered path over another plank bridge and a stile, continuing with the hedgerow to the L and, at the end of the field, go over another stile and plank bridge. Keep to the LHFE, ignoring the FPs to L and R until, a few yards further you reach a Y-junction of paths, where you keep L to head into a wooded area. You'll need to keep your wits about you as the EW signage here is woefully scant.

7) Pass the gate to the R, (you may recall this is where, earlier, we turned off into the forest near the start of the walk) and continue SA, out of the woods and, after a few yards TL through a wooden kissing gate. After another few yards squeeze, like moles in a trap, through a series of 4 alarming metal "rambler" gates, then finally a reassuringly old-fashioned wooden gate to TR onto the RHFE. Head slightly downhill to reach the road. Cross the road to take the FP almost SA, across the plank bridge, heading toward Greensted. Then cross another plank bridge to reach the lane. TR to walk up to the church (and, if you're lucky, a friendly pig en route). Dating from the 11th century, St Andrews is the oldest wooden church in the world and probably the oldest standing wooden building in Europe.

Fishing lake

The Green Man, Toot Hill

St Andrews Church, Greensted

THE ESSEX WAY IN CIRCULAR WALKS

3: Greensted to Witney Green

Total distance: 8 miles

Of which Essex Way: 4 miles

Map: OS Explorer 183 (TL 572 067)

Parking: The walk starts at the Church of St Nicholas, Willingale Road, Fyfield, CM5 0SB. You can park, with consideration, on the road outside the church.

Pubs on route: The Forresters Arms, The Street, High Ongar; The Cock Tavern, High Street, Chipping Ongar; The Kings Head, High Street, Chipping Ongar.

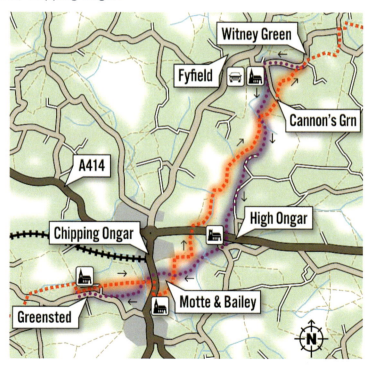

25

Walk Overview

The walk begins at the village of Fyfield and takes us cross-country on the Three Forests Way through High Ongar and Chipping Ongar. We pass the earthworks of a medieval motte and bailey castle and join the Essex Way at the historic Greensted Church. We then meander alongside the River Roding to Witney Green.

Directions

1) As you look at the church, take the FP to the R to walk along a track and then through a metal gate into a field. Cross the field, keeping the river to the R and a row of houses to the L. At the end of the row of houses and at a gap in the trees, take the FP on the R, through the trees. Once through the trees, continue SA across the field and over a plank bridge into the next field.

2) At the end of the field and a junction of FPs continue SA to cross over the EW, then cross a short grassy strip to another marker post. Go over a ditch to join the Three Forests Way, which we will now be following for the first half of the walk. Keep the river on the R, then go over a plank bridge, cross the next field and then keep to the RHFE with the woods to the R. Go through the trees, passing a small lake on the R, to reach some hard-standing to walk between the buildings of Little Forest Hall and on to a tarmac track.

3) At Little Forest Cottages on the L, leave the tarmac path and take the FP to the R across the field toward a house surrounded by a dense yew hedge. At West Park Lodge continue on Forest Lane and, part way down this road, TR onto the FP to continue on the Three Forests Way through the trees, then TL to walk along the LHFE heading toward the road. At the end of the tree line on the L, continue SA toward the church. Go over a stile and down some steps, cross this busy road with care, then climb the steps and the stile the other side and cross the meadow to go through the pub car park. TR to walk through High Ongar village. Pass the church (we found a tiny colourful piece of puddingstone in the church wall here. If you're new to the joys of the puddingstone, check out our book *Puddingstone Walks in Essex*) and TL into Mill Lane. Take the FP on the R to walk between the houses to open fields, passing school playing fields on the R and continuing downhill toward the river.

4) Cross the bridge and TL, keeping the river on the L, to walk along the LHFE, then follow the FP to the R away from the river, keeping to the RHFE. After a few yards, at the signage, take the diagonal L across the field. On reaching a grassy track running across, TL and, after a few yards, TR through a wooden kissing gate, following the signage for the "Permissive Route to Ongar Castle", the remains of a 12th century motte and bailey castle that was occupied until the 16th century. You can still see the overgrown mound of the motte to the L as we circumnavigate it. Go through another wooden kissing gate on the L to walk through the library car park to reach Chipping Ongar High Street. TL past the library and The Cock Tavern.

5) Cross the road to take Banson's Lane, walking past Sainsbury's on the L. Cross the river (in which we observed the obligatory dumped shopping trolley – admittedly this isn't the prettiest part of the walk, but bear with it, it gets better) and take the FP on the L. On reaching the houses, TR to walk along Millbank Avenue. At the end of the road, take the FP ahead, to walk between houses. Continue along the LHFE and, at the end of the field, TL to follow the FP over a stile and then TR onto the road. After around 200yds, TR into Church Lane, making for the 11th century Greensted Church, the oldest wooden church in the world and probably the oldest standing wooden building in Europe.

6) TR to join the EW. Follow the EW signs into the field, passing paddocks on the R, and cross a plank bridge to walk between fields with views of Chipping Ongar ahead. Arrive once again at Chipping Ongar High Street, then TR. Cross the road and TR, passing the Kings Head on the R. At the Ongar village sign TL and pass the 11th century St Martin's Church, thought to have once contained the cell of an anchorite (a curious sort of religious hermit, apparently). Walk through the alley to reach the road, then TL through a wooden kissing gate to walk along the LHFE and follow the path to the L then R to pass the Motte and Bailey on the L. While experiencing a brief sense of déjà-vu, follow the path SA then round to the R, keeping the children's playground to the L.

7) On reaching the next field, TR to walk along the RHFE, downhill. At the bottom of the field TL just after the hedge to walk with the woods on the R and the hedge on the L on a broad grassy track. At the edge of the woods, take a diagonal R to head for the gap in the hedge to the road. From here we spotted some woolly alpacas and idle donkeys in the farm to the R. Go up the steps, cross the busy road with caution, go down the steps the other side and TR. Walking parallel with road on the R for a few yards, you'll reach some woefully misleading signage. Ignore the signage - that way madness lies - as the path ahead is impassable (which we found to our cost after getting comically snarled up in the undergrowth). So, instead, TL at the signage to continue along the fence-line until you reach the road.

8) Cross the road and take the path SA into the field, then take the path diagonally R across the field. Follow the FP round to the L, keeping the hedgerow on the L. Then, at the end of the field, cross a single plank bridge. The EW signage is poor here. TL to keep the river on the R. Work your way round the fallen crack willows and over a series of 3 plank bridges, for a long peaceful meander along the riverside. Ignore the next plank bridge on the R, then cross a series of 6 further bridges, which have been thoughtfully supplied by the Ramblers, then finally a metal pontoon bridge. Cross the bridge and TL, then TR into a covered path, (which we found quite soggy in the winter), for a few hundred yards to reach a lane. Notice the delightful wooden, thatched carriage on the L.

9) Continue SA for a few yards, then on the bend take the FP to the R opposite the huff-style house, to enter a covered path. On reaching the road, **TL to leave the EW** and walk along the road back to the church.

Cottages at High Ongar

Thatched railway carriage

Fallen willow

THE ESSEX WAY IN CIRCULAR WALKS

4: **Witney Green to Peppers Green**

Total distance: **7.5** miles

Of which Essex Way: 3.5 miles

Map: OS Explorer 183 (TL 602 099)

Parking: The walk starts in the car parking area opposite Berners Hall Farm, Berners Roding, CM5 0TB.

Pubs on route: None, alas.

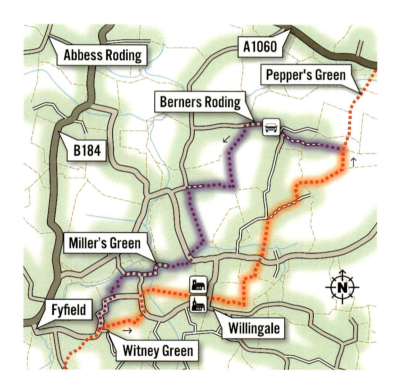

Walk Overview

The first part of the walk takes us from Berners Roding across wide open fields with striking views all around. We join the Essex Way at Witney Green and then it's on to the twin churches of Willingale and some pretty green lanes back to Berners Roding.

Directions

1) Walk back down the lane the way you came in and take the FP to the L opposite Berners Hall Farm, crossing the plank bridge to head diagonally R across the field towards a thicket. Once across the field, continue SA on a broad, grassy track, passing the thicket on the L, then keeping to the RHFE. At the end of the field, at the junction of FPs, TL to walk along the LHFE. At the end of the field make a quick R and L to cross the ditch into the next field, then cross over the next field to make for the tree line and the metal railings of a plank bridge. Cross the bridge then TR to walk along a covered track.

2) Follow the track round until you happen upon a surprising oasis of well-tended shrubs and the delightful Grade II listed Elm Cottage, then continue on the track past the cottage. As the lane bends to the R, take the FP to the L to walk along the RHFE. At the end of the field, cross the plank bridge into the next field, then cross the next field, noticing the views of the surrounding countryside from this high spot.

3) Cross yet another plank bridge and the next field. At the T-junction of paths at the end of the field TR to head for the lane. At the end of the field, TL through the gap in the trees and TL onto the lane. Just after McKerros, take the FP on the R to continue on the RHFE, following alongside McKerros on the R. You will notice the tower and spire of the twin churches of Willingale across to the L. Follow the field round as it twists and turns, alongside a small stream behind the trees on the R.

4) On reaching the fence-line bounding a large garden, TL to cross a plank bridge to the L, then TR to continue along the RHFE, passing a white house on the R. After a short while, you'll reach a lane, opposite the very charming Charley Farm and a ford. TL onto the lane and follow it round passing Hyde Cottage on the L. Pass the Willingale/Millers Green junction and, after 100yds or so, take the FP to the L. Cross the field slightly diagonally R towards the telegraph pole, and straight on, through a gap in the hedge, then TL onto the LHFE. After a few yards at the fingerpost TR to head across the field towards the hedgerow. Once across the field TL, keeping to the RHFE. Go through the wooden kissing gate and TR onto the road, passing Alders Farm on the R. (We spotted a cluster of deer here in the field on the R). Follow the road as it bends round, passing the intriguingly named Radar House on the R.

5) At Witney Green and Coach House, go through the gate on the L **to join the EW.** Head diagonally L across the paddock to a wooden gate and head across the field. At the end of the field, go through the hedgerow to continue across the next field. Cross the plank bridge to the lane and TL onto the lane. At the junction at Millers Green Road continue SA for a few yards, then take the FP to the R to cross a plank bridge and then immediately TL to walk along the LHFE opposite Hill House. Follow the fence round to the L and then TR at an apparently handmade EW sign to head across the field, slightly downhill, to cross a plank bridge over a little stream. TL to skirt the RHFE and then, at the mystifying FPS with multiple markers on it, continue uphill keeping to the LHFE, passing a pretty thatched house over the field to the L. Go uphill gradually as the white spire and square tower of the two churches of Willingale hove into view.

6) At the end of the field, cross a plank bridge to the L and TR to head up towards the two churches of Willingale. (The older of the two, St Andrew's, with the spire, dates from the 12th century. The larger of the two, St Christopher's, was built in the 14th century, probably to accommodate the increasing population as the wool industry flourished here). Enter the churchyard and walk through to exit it again via the gate. Cross the road and take the FP opposite through a small alleyway to a sports field. Continue along the RH edge and through into the next field. At the 2nd gap on the R, TR to cross the ditch, then TL, keeping to the LHFE. At the end of the field, TL across the plank bridge, and continue along the RHFE. At the end of the field TR through the hedge and TL to continue on the LHFE. Follow the field edge round, then TL to cross a plank bridge and continue SA on the LHFE.

7) Cross the road and continue SA, to enter a shady covered track. At the end of the path, TR onto a lane. After a while TL onto the byway before Rowe's Farm to walk along a covered path. Continue on this path, ignoring the junction of paths at the plank bridge on the R. After a few hundred yards, where the path bends to the L, follow the EW to the L to stay on the path through the trees. At the next junction of FPs, **we leave the EW** to TL to walk along the RHFE. Continue on this path all the way back to Berners Hall Farm.

Elm Cottage

Cottage near Miller's Green

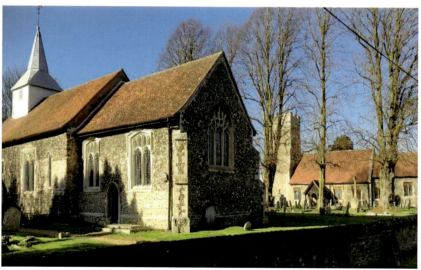
Twin churches of Willingale

THE ESSEX WAY IN CIRCULAR WALKS

5: Peppers Green to Round Roblets

Total distance: **6.5** miles

Of which Essex Way: **3** miles

Map: OS Explorer 183 (TL 624 122)

Parking: The walk starts at the Village Hall in Good Easter, School Road, CM1 4RT. There is some parking space outside the hall or else you can park, with consideration, in the surrounding streets.

Pubs on route: None, alas.

Walk Overview

The walk starts at the small peaceful village of Good Easter, erstwhile home of horticulturalist Beth Chatto. After a walk along a lane and across open fields, we head into the quiet green lanes of the Essex Way. We pass the tiny hamlet of Peppers Green, then on through the churchyard of St Andrews, past Farmbridge End to Round Roblets, where we leave the Essex Way to take the lane back to Good Easter.

Directions

1) Keeping the village hall on the L, walk down the road towards High Easter, passing the School House on the R, sporting an appropriately-themed weather vane. Follow the road downhill for around a third of a mile, ignoring the first FP on the L and, where the road bends round to the R, take the lane to the L. At the pretty thatched Graylings, take the path SA to the R to walk beside the ford. Cross the concrete bridge to the L to continue along the lane. Where the road bends R take the FP to the L to cross a broad grassy track between fields.

2) Just before the lake, in spite of the lack of signage, TR to circumnavigate it in an anticlockwise direction until you reach a FP to the R. Take this FP to walk along the LHFE until you reach the road. Cross the road onto the pavement, then TL for a few yards and, just past Hunts Cottage, take the FP to the R keeping to the RHFE. On reaching the next field at the crossroads of FPs, continue SA across the field, heading for the trees. At the end of the field cross two plank bridges then TR to keep to the RHFE with the trees on your R. At the end of the field cross the ditch (alas no plank bridge here) and continue to follow the yellow-topped marker posts, go over the plank bridge and cross the next field. At the end of the field cross the plank bridge and then cross the next field.

3) Once across the field, TL along the LHFE to reach a track, to **join the EW.** TL onto this shady path, eventually following it round past Old Cris Field and the other cottages of Peppers Green, where the path becomes a tarmacked lane. Continue to the road and cross the road, (noticing the EW signage bearing the three-seax coat of arms of the county of Essex) to take the FP opposite. Continue on this path to eventually reach a tarmacked lane at Ladyland, then continue SA to reach the road.

4) At the junction at Bridge House, TL to walk over the bridge and, after a short while, take the FP to the L. Go through the trees and follow the path round to the L, keeping to the LHFE. Cross the plank bridge and TR keeping to the RHFE. Follow the path across the field, heading for the church. Notice the beautiful half-timbered house across to the R. Cross the plank bridge into the churchyard of St Andrews, with its charming timber belfry, and follow the path L round the church to exit the churchyard through the gate. TL onto the road, passing the undulating Barns of Falcons Hall.

5) At the junction TR towards Pleshey, passing Forge End on the L. At the picture-perfect Primrose Cottage, TL onto the FP and then TR onto a broad grassy track to pass behind some pretty cottages. At the end of the field TL at the FPS to walk along the RHFE. At the end of the field, cross the plank bridge and TR onto the lane. Just after a bend to the R, take the unsignposted FP on the R through the trees to **leave the EW.**

6) Once through the trees, go SA passing farm buildings, piggy smells and squeals on the R, heading for the FPS in the trees slightly diagonally L. Cross the plank bridge and continue through the trees and over a stile (here be goats) then on to the lane at Round Roblets. TR and follow this quiet country lane through the hamlet of Tye Green and back to Good Easter.

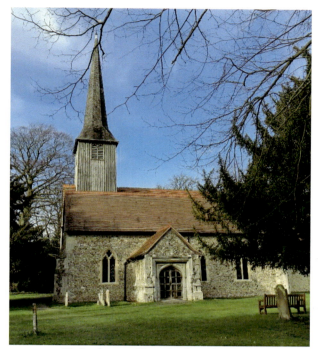
St Andrews Church, Good Easter

Half-timbered house

Lake near Fouchers House

Undulating barns of Falcons Hall

THE ESSEX WAY IN CIRCULAR WALKS

6: Round Roblets to Pleshey

Total distance: 7.5 miles

Of which Essex Way: 4 miles

Map: OS Explorer 183 (TL 665 145)

Parking: The walk starts at The Leather Bottle, The Street, Pleshey, CM3 1HG. You can park, with consideration, on the surroundings streets.

Pubs on route: The Leather Bottle, The Street, Pleshey.

Walk Overview

Pleshey is a surprisingly understated and peaceful little village, despite hosting the ruins of an 11th century motte and bailey castle in its midst that boasts one of the highest mottes in England. We start the walk by circumnavigating part of the earthworks of the castle, then go cross-country to the intriguingly named Round Roblets where we pick up the Essex Way. Then it's a stroll through green lanes back to Pleshey, with a glimpse of the castle moat and some charming listed buildings.

Directions

1) With your back to the pub TL to walk down the road passing Back Lane on the L. As the road bends to the L, take the FP on the L and follow it round to the L, circumnavigating the raised earthwork of the ancient motte and bailey castle. Go through the avenue of trees to reach a field and continue, keeping to the LHFE. Cross the lane and continue on the FP SA. Cross the plank bridge and take the FP to the R to walk along the RHFE. At the end of the field TL briefly onto the EW and, after around 50yds, leave the EW to take the FP to the R.

2) Follow this path round to the L to keep to the LHFE. After a short while go through the hedge into the next field, continuing on the LHFE, then take the FP to the L, keeping to the L of the wooden fencing to follow the path round to the R as it takes you through the grounds of a property (at the time of writing the landowner told us he had applied for the FP to be rerouted round the property). Cross a plank bridge then TL onto the road then, at the bend in the road, look out for a FP on the R.

3) TR onto the FP to double back on yourself, keeping to the RHFE, behind some houses and stylishly converted barns, then TL onto the track. Just after the corrugated barn, take the FP on the R and pick your way through to the L of the barn then continue SA keeping to the LHFE. Take the FP on the L through the hedgerow to walk through a meadow and, after 70yds TR back through the hedgerow, then TL keeping to the LHFE. At the corner of the field follow the FPS round to the L. Just before the plank bridge TR following round the LHFE. Cross the plank bridge into the next field and continue SA toward the houses. TL onto the road and, at the long, thatched Beam Ends, take the FP on the R over a plank bridge, keeping to the LHFE. At the corner of the field, before another plank bridge, TL to walk along the RHFE. At the end of the field TR onto a broad track to walk to a junction of paths. Cross the field ahead, slightly diagonally R to head towards the 3 low barn rooftops.

4) Cross the plank bridge and TR to walk along the RHFE. At the corner of the field TL to continue on the RHFE toward the barns. Cross the farm track and take the path SA to the R of the corrugated barns. Follow the path round the back of the barns and continue on the LHFE. At the end of the field make a quick R and then L through the trees into the next field and follow round on the LHFE. At the end of the field cross the track and go SA with the lake to the R and quickly TL through an area of scrubland. Pick your way round the farm buildings to reach the small lane and TL up the lane passing Round Roblets on the L, then TR at the road junction.

5) Almost immediately, take the FP on the R, go over a stile, through a copse and over a plank bridge. Once through the copse continue SA passing farm buildings on the L then cross scrubland with a very piggy whiff, heading for a FPS in the gap in the treeline ahead. Go SA through a covered path to the road. **TR onto the lane to join the EW,** although you won't see any EW signage for a while.

6) Where the road bends to the R, TL onto a track for a brief spell. Where the path bends round to the L go through the gate and TR to follow the EW signs, walking alongside a paddock and, after a while, go through a metal gate onto a covered path. Continue on this path for an enjoyable long stroll until you reach the lane. TR onto the lane at Stagdon Cross, and pass the handsome timbered farmhouse on the L. Pass the road on the L to Barnston and Dunmow and continue toward Pleshey, Mashbury and Chelmsford. After a while take the byway on the L. (Where the path opens out, we spotted a large muster of deer in the fields across to the R - we counted at least 20). Eventually join a concrete track passing Woods Farm on the R and, at the junction, TR. Ignore the first FP on the R and, after a while, take the bridleway to the R opposite Blakes Lane. Continue on this broad shady path ignoring FPs to L and R until reaching the road.

7) TL onto the road to walk through the village passing on the R the Holy Trinity Church, with its cute side-minaret, and some stunning listed buildings, as well as part of the castle moat, best seen at the beautiful Pleshey Mount View Point. The castle is in now in private ownership, so can be visited by appointment only. However, if you pop up Pump Lane, you can have a quick look at the brick bridge that formed the entry to the castle before returning to the start of the walk.

Rose Cottage, Pleshey

Avenue of trees

A muster of deer

THE ESSEX WAY IN CIRCULAR WALKS

7: Pleshey to Chatham Green

Total distance: 8 miles

Of which Essex Way: 3.5 miles

Map: OS Explorer 183 (TL 716 150)

Parking: The walk starts at the free car parking area off the A131 just before The Windmill Inn, Chatham Green, Little Waltham, Chelmsford, CM3 3LE.

Pubs on route: The Windmill Inn, Chatham Green; The Beehive, Barrack Lane, Great Waltham.

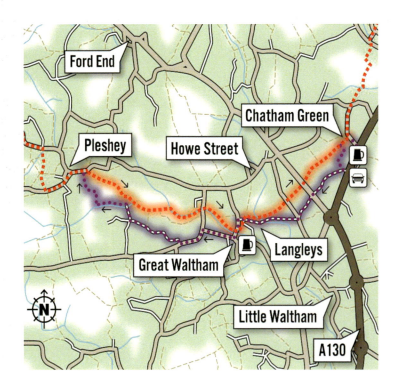

Walk Overview

The first part of the walk takes us along green lanes and open fields and across the River Chelmer to the impressive Langleys, and on via Great Waltham to the outskirts of Pleshey. We then take a very pleasant stretch of the Essex Way along Walthambury Brook and open fields to Chatham Green.

Directions

1) TL out of the car park and pass The Windmill pub on the L. Just after Little Longs, take the EW FP on the L. Continue on this green covered path then TL to leave the EW and walk along the RHFE. Cross the plank bridge on the R and keep to the RHFE. At the end of the field continue to follow the RHFE round to the L, TR onto the lane and follow it all the way to the road. Cross the road and continue on the tarmacked track SA. At the junction TL for a few yards then take the FP to the R (where we pick up the EW for a bit) to pass a lodge, then go all the way up to the river bridge.

2) Cross the river, enjoy the bubbly weir and pass Langleys on your L, a fine early 18th century red-bricked house. Continue along the drive, past the pet cemetery on the L, then between inquisitive cows and lollipopped trees. Before reaching the road, TL through the 1st of 4 rusty old kissing gates to walk across the meadow. Exit via the 2nd rusty gate, cross the drive, then enter the next paddock, through the 3rd rusty gate. Cross the next paddock to Great Waltham, briefly picking up a section of the Saffron Trail. Exit the meadow and the EW via the 4th rusty gate. TL onto the road to walk down through the village. TR up Barrack Lane, passing The Beehive. At the junction, follow the Mashbury Road round to L, toward The Chignalls, Mashbury and The Easters.

3) Ignore the first FP to the R then, after around 100yds, take the next unmarked FP to the R, between two concrete blocks. Follow this broad grassy track round to the L, all the way up to the charming

Fitzjohn's Farm. At the junction take the R fork then, after a couple of yards, at the next junction of 3 paths, take the middle one to go SA keeping to the RHFE, heading slightly downhill, with a view of Pleshey Church on the horizon to the L. Just before the bottom of the field, take the plank bridge to the R then TL following the track as it winds downhill. On reaching the field, TL to walk along the LHFE. Cross the plank bridge and go SA along the LHFE, with Pleshey Church in the distance ahead.

4) At the field corner, take the FP to the R to stay on the LHFE. At around the high point of the field, take the unmarked track to the L, heading between fields towards farm buildings. Ahead of you, notice the grassy mound or "motte" of Pleshey Castle that features in Walk 6. At the corner of the field take the FP to the R, keeping to the LHFE, and eventually go through a metal gate. Just before reaching the road, look to the R where you'll find an EW FPS beside some metal gates.

5) **Take this FP to begin our section of the EW** and walk along the boundary fence of the water treatment works, then keep to the LHFE. Ignore the first plank bridge on the L and, after a while, the path takes you across a brook and keeps to the RHFE for a long agreeable stroll beside the brook. At the end of the woods, where the concrete path crosses the brook to the R, TL to walk uphill between fields to the corner of the raised bank of a reservoir (the signage is poor here). On reaching the reservoir, TR to walk along the LHFE. At the end of the reservoir, bear R to keep to the LHFE. Just before another reservoir, TR onto a track and follow it until it winds round to the L, then stay R to keep to the R of the reservoir. Follow this broad grassy track, with the brook on the R, to the road. Cross the road and go SA along the LHFE.

6) Cross the next road and take the FP SA, to go through a rusty kissing gate. Try not to be alarmed by the "Bull in Field" sign before experiencing some brief déjà vu as we retrace some of our earlier steps for a short while, passing through 3 more familiar rusty kissing

gates, before we finally TR onto the drive back up to Langleys. Follow the path round to the L keeping North Lodge on the L to go over the river. Keep the river on the right then cross the next bridge with white wooden rails. Déjà vu over now, veer off the path to the L to go through yet another rusty kissing gate onto a broad grassy track. After a while, cross the road and take the FP opposite to keep to the LHFE. Cross the main road with care and take the FP ahead to walk along the LHFE. Go through the hedgerow into the next field, staying on the LHFE. Cross the plank bridge into the next field and continue on the LHFE, then take the covered path and shortly **TR onto the lane to leave the EW** and head back to the car park.

The weir at Langleys

Langleys

Rape fields in the spring

THE ESSEX WAY IN CIRCULAR WALKS

8: Chatham Green to Fuller Street

Total distance: 6 miles

Of which Essex Way: 3.5 miles

Map: OS Explorer 183 (TL 747 160)

Parking: The walk starts at The Square and Compasses, Fuller Street, Fairstead, CM3 2BB. The pub has a car park for patrons. Others can park on the street nearby.

Pubs on route: The Square and Compasses, Fuller Street, Fairstead; The Windmill Inn, Chatham Green.

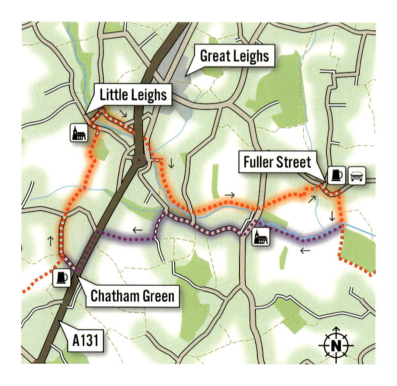

Walk Overview

The walk starts with a brief section of Essex Way at Fuller Street (featured in Walk 9), before a peaceful riverside walk, then on to Chatham Green, where we pick up the Essex Way again. We pass through the delightful village of Little Leighs and back along the river to Fuller Street.

Directions

1) With your back to the pub, TL to walk to the junction, passing the phone box that's been turned into an Essex Way information point on the R and the Victorian post box in the wall on the L. TL and walk for around 100yds, then take the EW FP on the R between houses. Follow this path as it doglegs to R and L then keep to the LHFE. Follow the field edge round, past the first FP on the L and continue on the EW and then TL alongside the stream on the L and shortly cross a plank bridge. Go SA and, after 25yds, leave the EW to take the FP to the R.

2) Continue alongside a barbed wire fenced paddock, keeping the stream to the R, eventually passing through some woods, where we were enchanted by a sea of bluebells in the springtime. Exit the woods and keep the fencing to the L, go through two metal kissing gates for a pleasing stroll along the River Ter, which takes you past some very inquisitive cows, across 2 plank bridges and a meadow to exit via a stile onto the road. TL and pass the Church of St Mary, with its very exquisite round Norman tower, (one of only six round towers in Essex and the 3rd largest in the country). You can also find a piece of puddingstone in the L side of the tower around chest height. (If you're interested in puddingstones, check out our book *Puddingstone Walks in Essex*). Walk the few yards down to the junction and take Goodmans Lane on the R, passing the, now defunct, thatched water pump, for a fair amble along this peaceful lane, which passes the beautifully kept grounds of Hole Farm on the R and Goodman's Hall on the L.

3) Pass Paulk Hall Lane on the R and continue to follow the lane until the road bends to the R just before the bridge. TL at the huge chestnut tree onto an unmarked FP, then continue on the RHFE, ignoring the track to the R, and eventually take the 1st FP on the R, to go through a covered path then, at the crossroads, TL onto a dirt track. After 25yds take the FP to the R then immediately R again to cross the ditch and TL to keep to the LHFE. Around ⅔ of the way along the field, take the plank bridge on the L, then go through the next field, keeping to the RHFE.

4) Exit, with a rude awakening, onto the noisy A131. (Please excuse this short section of main road – it's necessary to avoid too circuitous a route to the EW section of our walk, and you will be rewarded with some lovely sights soon). TL to walk along the verge, until you reach the 2nd traffic island. Cross here, then TL and, after a short while, TR up Chatham Green Lane. Continue up the lane, passing The Windmill Inn on the L. Just after Little Longs, the road becomes part of the EW.

5) We are now on the EW section of the walk. Follow the road round to the R through Chatham Green and, at the junction, go SA on a concrete track, through a wooden gate into the *Wilderness*. Walk through the *Wilderness* and out again through a wooden gate and continue SA on the RHFE. At the bottom of the field TL, continuing on the RHFE then, at the end of the field, TR at the two-way EW sign, to walk along the green path, passing a large fishing lake on the R, through to the lane. TL, pass the church on the L then TR up Rectory Lane. Go over the bridge and through the surprisingly delightful hamlet of Little Leighs, with its quaint chocolate box cottages. TR onto White Lane (we saw a few jays flitting in and out of the trees here), then go through the underpass.

6) Cross the next road and go over a stile then down steps to a field. TR to walk along the RHFE, with the stream to the R, go over a plank bridge and then past the water treatment works on the L. Go through the trees into a field, keeping to the RHFE, then through a wooden gate to walk across a meadow. If you interpret the confusing signage correctly, you will go over the stile to the L, and immediately TR to walk along the RHFE, keeping to the L of barbed wire fencing, still following the line of the river until you reach a lane. TR and, after a few yards, take the FP to the L to walk up some steps, through a wooden gate and immediately TR, keeping the fence to the R and observing the curious tumble-down barn in the meadow to the L. Exit through another wooden gate to the next meadow and, at the end of this paddock, go over a plank bridge and stile to a horsy paddock. (A warning - as you approach the road, don't head straight for the gate, but keep to the R to walk near to the river, then work your way round to the gate. The higher ground is alarmingly swampy, and we've come a cropper in the past. (In fact, we ended up so sodden and caked in mud up to the knees that we had to postpone our lunch appointment at The Square and Compasses).

7) Go over the stile, cross the road and take the FP straight ahead, beside the enclosed spring (one of a number that feed the River Ter). Follow the track for a few yards before veering off to the L across the field (we found ourselves walking between vivid yellow walls of rape in the springtime). At the end of the field go through the hedge and veer to the L then under some power lines, keeping to the LHFE, with the village and pub across to the R. At the marker post TR to head across the field toward the road. You may spot some woolly alpacas in a garden across to the R. On reaching the road TR, then TL at the junction to return to the pub.

Bluebell woods

Rose Cottage, Little Leighs

Fishing lake at Little Leighs

THE ESSEX WAY IN CIRCULAR WALKS

9: Fuller Street to Fairstead

Total distance: **4.5** miles

Of which Essex Way: 3.5 miles

Map: OS Explorer 183 (TL 767 167)

Parking: The walk starts at St Mary the Virgin Church, Fairstead Hall Road, Fairstead, CM3 2AT. You can park, with consideration, on the road outside.

Pubs on route: The Square and Compasses, Fuller Street, Fairstead.

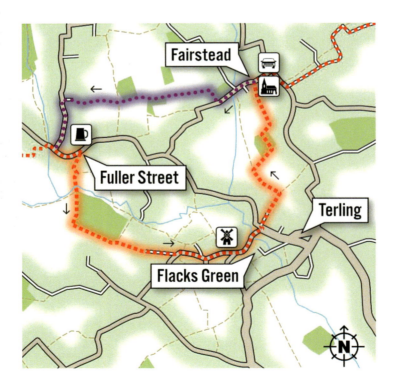

Walk Overview

A short walk in which we stay on the Essex Way for almost three quarters of the route. From Fairstead Church we take a gentle walk across open countryside and alongside woods and hedgerows teeming with wildlife, to Fuller Street where we pick up the Essex Way. The pretty village of Terling, with its smock mill and ford, is en route and then it's through covered paths and tranquil woods back to Fairstead.

Directions

1) With your back to the church, TL to walk down the hill, passing Fairstead Hall Farm and ignoring the first FPs to R and L. At the end of the treeline to the R, take the FP to the R. Follow the RHFE to the end of the field, with the treeline on the R. At the end of the field TL, keeping to the RHFE with the hedgerow on the R. At the corner of the field, TR through the gap in the hedge, then continue L on a broad sward along the LHFE. Pass under the power lines to the marker post at the corner of the wooded area and continue on the RHFE. (We saw a red kite and a buzzard circling together here).

2) Cross a plank bridge to the next field and continue SA through the field heading towards farm buildings. Enjoy the peacefulness of this lovely open countryside, broken only by the piercing cry of the peacocks (or peahens) in the nearby farm. (In fact we were beset with a wide array of fauna here – an assortment of wildfowl on the path, a drove of 8 hares playing in the field and a muntjac bouncing past, all accompanied by the sound of a springtime cuckoo). Pick your way through the farm buildings of Fairstead Lodge to the gravel path and on to the road, then TL. Pass some sweet cottages before reaching the Square and Compasses and the **start of our section of the EW.**

3) Walk to the junction, passing the phone box that's been turned into an Essex Way information point on the R and the Victorian post box in the wall on the L. TL and walk for around 100yds, then take the EW FP on the R between houses. Follow this path as it doglegs to R and L then keep to the LHFE. Follow the field edge round, past the first FP on the L and after a while TL, continuing on the LHFE and shortly cross a plank bridge. Go SA, keeping Sandy Wood to the L and passing under power lines. In the spring, you can see a magnificent display of bluebells here. At the end of the woods TL onto the track, keeping to the LHFE, and continue SA to the end of the woods along a broad green sward. At the next corner of the woods, TL to continue along the green path and then TR through the field.

4) Once over the field, continue SA with the paddock on the L and onto a small track that takes you out to a tarmacked lane and some sweet cottages at Terling. Ignoring FPs to R and L, continue past the phone box on the L and, at the junction, TL to continue up Hull Lane. As you pass Mill Lane on the L, look out for the Grade II listed smock windmill, c1818. At the next junction notice the unusual brick pillar Georgian post box before you TL onto Norman Hill. Follow the road downhill then cross the ford (or pause awhile for your picnic on the bench at this pretty spot) then, at the junction, cross the road and make a quick L and R to take the FP SA on a tarmac track. Pass a farm and follow the path L on the RHFE.

5) At the corner of the field TL, continuing on the RHFE. At the bottom corner of the field TR into the next field for a few yards, then TL and walk up to the finger post at the next field, then TR to walk along the RHFE. At the end of the field, walk onto a broad grassy track with a wooded area to the L and, just before the end of the woods, TL into the trees, taking the path through tranquil woods. Once out of the woods TR on the RHFE. At the corner of the field TL to make for the church, go over a plank bridge, cross the field and go through a covered path then another plank bridge to the R. TL between the gravestones and return to the church.

Terling Smock Mill

Springtime fields at Fuller Street

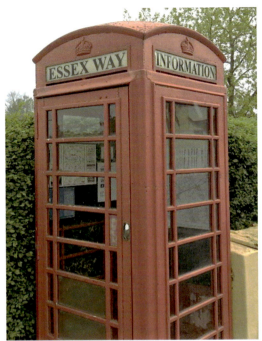

Essex Way Information Point

The ford at Terling

THE ESSEX WAY IN CIRCULAR WALKS

10: Fairstead to White Notley

Total distance: 6 miles

Of which Essex Way: 3 miles

Map: OS Explorer 183 (TL 785 183)

Parking: The walk starts at The Cross Keys Pub, 1 The Street, White Notley, CM8 1RQ You can park, with consideration, on the surrounding streets or in the pub car park if you are using the pub.

Pubs on route: The Cross Keys, The Street, White Notley.

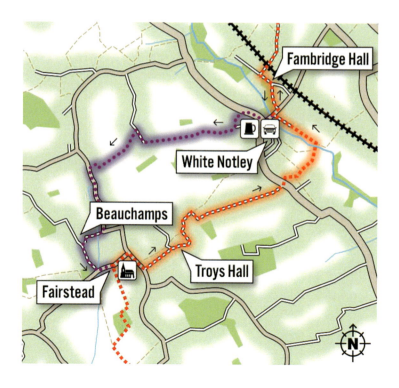

61

Walk Overview

From the village of White Notley our walk takes us across open farmland and quiet country lanes where we join the Essex Way at Fairstead. Then it's along tree-lined paths and covered walks to pick up a section of the John Ray Walk for a peaceful saunter beside the River Brain.

Directions

1) With your back to the pub, TL to walk up the hill, passing some listed buildings on the R, one dated as early as 1711. Take the FP to the L opposite White Notley Village Hall. Follow the path to the L round the back of the black weather-boarded converted barns, then follow the FP to the R, noticing on the L the cheery flying pig weather-vane, to walk alongside a boundary wall.

2) As the path opens out, continue SA to join the RHFE and stay on the RHFE until eventually passing under some metal pylon-supported power lines and, shortly after, TR onto a concrete track. After a corrugated barn TL, staying on a concrete track, and then on to the RHFE. Eventually cross a plank bridge and briefly TR and then L to continue on the RHFE. On reaching the road TL. Follow this quiet country lane for around half a mile, passing under the power lines.

3) Where the road bends to the L at Beauchamps, take the track to the R. Follow the path round to the L in front of Beauchamps, with its admirably-kempt lawns, then TL onto the concrete track. On reaching the road, TL to walk up to the church. The bench outside provides an excellent picnic spot with views across the fields. Just past the church, ignore the EW FP on the R (that's the end of Walk 9), and continue along the lane. **This part of the lane becomes the start of our section of EW.**

4) At the road junction TR, passing the VR post-box in the wall. This is a peaceful spot, except for the cries of some local peacocks (or peahens). Ignore the first FP on the L and take the next one, marked EW. Stay on this track for a fair way, through tree-lined avenues and covered paths, passing Troy's Hall. Just before reaching a made-up track TR through metal gates to walk parallel to the track on the L, then TL onto the concrete track to continue along this tree-lined route until reaching farm buildings. On reaching the road, cross over with caution and TL, passing Forge Cottage on the R. At the front of the cottage, you can feast your eyes on an arch shaped puddingstone. (Puddingstones are naturally occurring conglomerate boulders, formed around 55 million years ago, and are so named because of their distinctive composition of colourful pebbles, resembling the cherries and currants in an old-fashioned plum pudding. There are a number in Essex, each with their own unique charm. For more information and some good walks see our book *Puddingstone Walks in Essex*).

5) TR at the FPS and follow the path round behind the cottage. On reaching the 5-bar gate, veer off the gravel path onto a broad green path behind the cottage. After a while, walk between fields down to a beautiful section of the River Brain. Cross the concrete bridge over the river and TL for a peaceful walk beside the river on the L, crossing two stiles. (This is also part of the John Ray Walk, named after the 17th century botanist born at Black Notley and regarded as the father of British Natural History, in spite of not being a household name, perhaps because his major works were written in Latin). Go through a metal kissing gate to reach the road.

6) At this point you have a choice. You can TL **to leave the EW** and return to the pub. Or you can TR to continue on to the point of the EW where we start Walk 11. (This involves walking an extra three quarters of a mile there and back. You will be rewarded by some peaceful countryside, a picturesque hall and, if you're lucky, some spotty pigs). If you've chosen to TR, after a few yards, take the FP on the L all the way up to Fambridge Hall. Then follow the EW and John Ray Walk downhill and along beside the river as far as the R turn that would take you to the railway bridge. You can now retrace your steps back past Fambridge Hall to the road, then TR to go over the ford and back to the village and the pub.

White Notley Puddingstone

Fambridge Hall

The Corbels of Haven Cottage

River Brain

THE ESSEX WAY IN CIRCULAR WALKS

11: White Notley to Bradwell

Total distance: **7.5** miles

Of which Essex Way: **4** miles

Map: OS Explorer 183 & 195 (TL 817 221)

Parking: The walk starts at The Holy Trinity Church, Bradwell Church Road, Bradwell-juxta-Coggeshall, CM77 8AN. You can park off the road beside the church.

Pubs on route: None, alas.

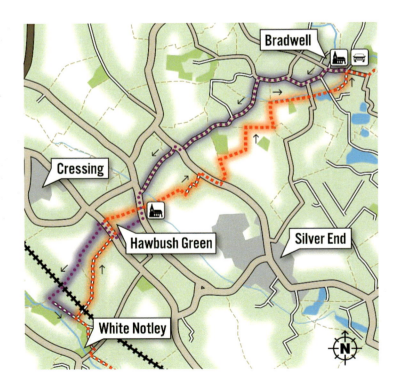

Walk Overview

This is a walk of two halves: part lanes, part fields and farmland. The first section takes us from Bradwell, along quiet country lanes to White Notley, where we pick up a very pretty section of the Essex Way. We ramble cross-country and then enjoy a shady woodland walk back to Bradwell.

Directions

1) Take the road opposite the church, signposted Silver End and Rivenhall. At the junction, keep R heading for Cressing. At the next junction, at Keeper's Cottage, TL. At the sweetly-named Periwinkle Hall TL to head for Cressing and Silver End. Stay on this quiet country lane for a while, passing some very pretty cottages and mature trees and hedgerow. On reaching the road TR for a few yards and then cross the road, with caution, and take the road on the L. At the end of the road, at the classic car showroom, cross over and TL.

2) After a few yards ignore the EW FP on the R (we'll be coming back through here later). Pass the church on the L and, after about 100yds, take the next unsignposted FP to the R, marked by some unwelcoming oil drums. Where the path opens out, continue on the RHFE and, on reaching the road, TR to walk along the pavement. Before the road bends to the L, cross the road and take the FP on the L to go through the hedge and TL to keep on the LHFE. Follow the field round to the R, keeping to the LHFE and heading for the pylons in the distance. Eventually cross a plank bridge at a gap in the hedge on the L and TR to continue on the RHFE.

3) On reaching the railway track, cross the stile and the tracks, with caution, then go over another stile into the field. TR to keep to the RHFE and follow the field edge downhill. At the bottom of the field TL along the track with the willow plantation on the R.

4) At the junction, take the L fork to pick up the EW. Walk under the railway bridge and continue on the track up to the farm, and then through to the road. Cross the road with caution and, with a brief sense of deja-vu, TL to walk along the pavement. Just before the road bends to the L, take the FP to the R into the trees, then beside fields until reaching another main road. Cross the road and TR for a few yards, then take the FP beside the church to walk along the LHFE until you reach the farm. Follow the path round the tidiest farmyard we've ever seen, passing a pretty lake, before reaching the road. TR, once again taking care and, after a short while, pass Wrights Farm on the L. A little further along TL onto the FP through the trees to a field, following the path round to the L to keep to the LHFE.

5) At the end of the treeline to the L, at the signage, TR to follow the EW with the ditch to your R, before reaching the woods ahead. (We saw hares in the field here in June). At the FPS, TL across the field, then TR to walk beside the hedge on the L. Go through the hedge ahead, following the LHFE and, at the end of this field, TL through the trees to continue on the RHFE.

6) At the bottom of the field (the signage is poor here) at a crossroads ahead and just before reaching the power lines TR, keeping to the LHFE with the ditch to your L and walking parallel with the power lines on the L. Eventually pass a copse on the R, (where we were enthralled by birdsong echoing around the treetops). On reaching the road TL for a few yards, then TR through the trees for a beautiful shady walk through the woods. You can just make out a lake through the trees on the R. Cross the quarry access road to head back into the bushes, following this pretty woodland path to emerge on to the road. **Leave the EW** and TL up the road to head back to the church.

Lakeside

Under the railway at White Notley

Green Lane

Cottage near Bradwell

THE ESSEX WAY IN CIRCULAR WALKS

12: Bradwell to Coggeshall

Total distance: 8.5 miles

Of which Essex Way: 4 miles

Map: OS Explorer 195 (TL 870 233)

Parking: The walk starts at the fishing lake beside Houchins Wedding Venue.

Pubs on route: The Woolpack Inn, Church Street, Coggeshall; The Chapel Inn, Market Hill, Coggeshall.

Walk Overview

Setting out from the 15th century farmhouse of Houchins, we take a stroll through open countryside, to the historic market town of Coggeshall, with its many timber-framed and listed buildings, including a Cistercian barn and an abbey, dating as far back as the 12th century.

Directions

1) Keeping the fishing lake to the R, walk up the path, passing the FPS for the EW on the L. At the end of the tarmac lane, continue SA on the farm track and onto the LHFE. At the field corner veer round to the L, then TR up a grassy path between two fields, heading towards farm buildings. Go through the hedgerow to continue on the path and, after a few yards, TL to walk along the LHFE. Proceed into the next field, taking the path between fields. Go through the hedge and down the steps to TL onto the lane. After a while, cross the busy A120 with caution and take the FP directly ahead through the trees to enter a residential area.

2) Pass Monkdowns Road on the R, TR at the T-junction and, after a few yards, TL up the FP to the L of the playground. Exit onto Beards Terrace and TR, then SA into the graveyard. Follow the path to exit the graveyard SA then TL, passing the allotments on the R. Pass the church on the L and TR out of the kissing gate and past the back of the Woolpack Inn on the L and then almshouses on the R. At the T-junction TL onto Vane Lane, then TR into Church Street to walk downhill passing many listed (and, indeed, listing) half-timbered buildings. At the junction TR into Stoneham Street, passing the Chapel Inn and The Clockhouse on the L. TL at the library, where Stoneham Street bends to the L. Take the FP to the R of the Millennium Garden, keeping the wall on the L. Go through this alley, over the concrete bridge and, on reaching the field, TL through a car park to West Street. (Notice the stunning half-timbered Paycockes over the road to the L, once the house and gardens of a wealthy Tudor cloth merchant and now owned by the National Trust). TR onto West Street.

3) Eventually pass the vineyard on the L and later Isinglass Mews on the R (once a factory in the mid-19th century making isinglass, a type of gelatine obtained mainly from sturgeons' air-bladders). At the football club take the FP on the L, follow the Public Right of Way signs through the car park and down the wooden steps into the water meadow. A pleasant walk beside the willow-lined River Blackwater ensues. Cross the river via the metal Dick Nunn's Bridge (named after an interesting local character and campaigner for working people who championed, amongst other things, public rights of way). Go SA through the scrub and, after a while, cross a plank bridge then go SA on the LHFE up to the lane. TR onto the EW briefly, then look out for a FPS in the hedge to the L, about 100yds before the farm ahead. Cross the field, then go across the next field and then TR onto the lane. There is a quarry to the L, being filled in at the time of writing. Further along the lane you may spot deer hiding among the sapling plantation on the R. Follow this winding country lane for around a mile, to reach the sign for Bradwell Trout Farm

4) This is where our section of the EW starts. At this point, if you wish to make sure you join up where Walk 11 ended, you can continue along the lane for a few yards to the start of the FP at the parking spot on the L opposite the metal gate, and then return to this point. Alternatively, start the EW here and TR toward the Trout Farm, where you can see an assortment of variegated animals through the fence, including miniature goats and alpacas. TR to walk alongside the fence, then continue along the LHFE, after a while passing the old quarry works on the R to eventually emerge onto a track which divides into two. Walk towards the R hand track and, almost immediately, TR onto the FP through the hedge to walk alongside the old quarry fence on the R. Eventually emerge on to a track, TR for a few yards then, at the T-junction, TL onto the lane to walk on the

RHFE for around a mile all the way up to the historic timber-framed Grange Barn, then out onto the road. (Grange Barn was built by Cistercian monks in the 13th century to serve Coggeshall Abbey. You may also notice an old petrol pump on the L a bit before this).

5) Cross the road and walk up Abbey Lane, passing on the L the 13th century St Nicholas Chapel, (once the gatehouse chapel to Coggeshall Abbey and the oldest post-Roman brick building in Essex). Also notice the EW milestone here, showing we've reached the halfway point of the EW. Pass the 12th century Coggeshall Abbey on the L, and the mill on the R, crossing the mill stream. At the T-junction of paths TL to walk with the paddock to the R, then cross over a concrete track, passing the Anglian Water building on the L, and go through a metal kissing gate. On reaching the road TL and, after a few yards, TR through the gate into the recreation ground. Ignore the path ahead and TR to walk around the edge of the ground with the hedge to the R, then go SA through an alley beside the school playing field to emerge onto the road opposite the church.

6) TR onto the road, passing redbrick almshouses on the R. At the junction TR to walk down St Peter's Road and, on reaching St Anne's Close on the R, take the FP on the L through the gate. Cross the field, then go through the hedge to cross into the next field keeping to the LHFE. Go up steps and be careful as you emerge onto the busy A120, cross the road and go down the steps the other side and over a stile to walk along the LHFE. Continue for half a mile or so, looking out for a FPS in the hedge to the L. Go through the hedge, down some steps and across a plank bridge. TR to walk along the RHFE to eventually emerge onto the lane and TR to return to the start of the walk.

Paycockes

Dick Nunn's Bridge

Mill stream

Coggeshall Abbey

Halfway point

THE ESSEX WAY IN CIRCULAR WALKS

13: Coggeshall to Great Tey

Total distance: **6.5** miles

Of which Essex Way: **3** miles

Map: OS Explorer 195 (TL 892 258)

Parking: The walk starts at St Barnabas Church, The Street, Great Tey, CO6 1JS. You can park in the street, with consideration.

Pubs on route: The Chequers, The Street, Great Tey.

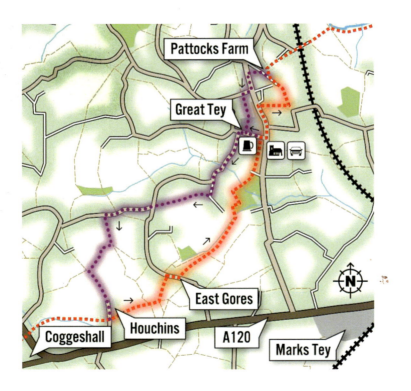

Walk Overview

The walk starts in the little rural parish of Great Tey, with its charming Norman church and quaint 16th century pub. From here we take country lanes and farmland to the 15th century Grade II listed Houchins, then on to East Gores and alongside woodland. We pass through Great Tey to take in a little more of the Essex Way before finally returning to the village.

Directions

1) With the church on your L walk along The Street, passing The Chequers on the L. Pass Greenfield Drive on the R and take the L turn signposted Coggeshall for around half a mile, ignoring the first FPs to R and L. Where the road bends round to the R, take the FP on the L before the house to walk along an unmade track. Just after a FP on the L across a field, take the FP on the R into a field, then immediately R to walk along the RHFE. At the field corner go SA across the fields all the way up to the road. TR briefly then take the road to the L signposted Coggeshall.

2) Pass the beautiful Bucklers Farm to the R and, just after Gulls Farm, ignore the bridleway on the L and take the FP also on the L just after it onto the LHFE. Go across a plank bridge and along the next LHFE. Part way along the field, where there is an incomplete marker post in the hedge, TR to cross the field (where a clear path had been cut through the crop in the summer). At the next field TL to follow round the LHFE to emerge onto a FP running across. TL through the hedge and walk along the broad grassy track between fields. Continue to follow the path on the RHFE all the way onto the lane at Houchins.

3) Our section of the EW begins when we pass the EW FP on the R Ignore this FP (we cover that in Walk 12) and, just past it, TL into the car park of the fishing lake. Walk along the track with the raised bank of the lake to the L and, where the track bends to the L, TR to take the grassy path on the LHFE (we saw a glorious purple sea of borage here in the summer). At the gap in the hedge TL into the next field then TR to continue on the RHFE. Follow the path round to the L onto to the LHFE to emerge onto the lane at East Gores.

4) TR onto the lane for a few yards and, just past Whytegate, take the FP to the L, eventually going along the LHFE. (We saw a red kite here). Continue SA past the curious wooden sign for Larry's Drive and onto the LHFE. Walk alongside the stream on the L. At the field corner cross a plank bridge and go through a metal kissing gate into the field. After a short while follow the marker posts through another metal kissing gate on the L and across a plank bridge and yet another kissing gate. Ignoring the misleading signage here (we think the post has been turned round), TR out of the gate and follow the RHFE round, keeping the woods on your R, and eventually go through another metal kissing gate to follow the path alongside the woods.

5) Exit the woods via a plank bridge and metal kissing gate and TR to walk along the RHFE with the woods to the R. Cross a culvert and enter a shady covered walk, passing a sewage farm on the R then go SA, keeping to the LHFE. Cross the track in front of the sliding metal gates on the L and into another covered path. Exit onto a green then TL to walk up to a gravel track, passing the church on the R, to emerge at Great Tey and The Chequers. TR onto the road, noticing the water pump on the L. At the road junction, cross over and TL, eventually passing Moors Road and, a bit further on, take the FP on the R at the white balustrades of Bellevue House to emerge onto the LHFE.

6) At the field corner TL through the hedgerow and onto the RHFE. At the next field corner TR down the steps through the treeline onto a covered path then TL. On reaching the farm fence bear L onto the farm track to leave the EW. Keep the fence to the R and, after a few yards, take the FP on the L, diagonally across the field. Cross the plank bridge and take care as you emerge onto the busy road. TL to walk into Great Tey then TR at the junction towards Earls Colne. Take the FP on the L across the field and into the playing field. Cross the playing field then go through the large trees to the alley and the road. TL then, after a short while, TR up Garden Fields and through the alley to return to the pub and the church.

Field of borage

Houchins

St Barnabas Church, Great Tey

The Chequers, Great Tey

14: Great Tey to Fordham

Total distance: **7.5** miles

Of which Essex Way: **3** miles

Map: OS Explorer 184 & 195 (TL 927 281)

Parking: The walk starts at The Three Horseshoes, 74 Church Road, Fordham, CO6 3NJ. You can park at the pub if you're drinking there, or else in the layby further along the road.

Pubs on route: The Three Horseshoes, Church Road, Fordham.

Walk Overview

From the village of Fordham, we traverse fields and farmland before picking up the Essex Way for a good stretch beside the River Colne to Ford Street. We pass through the lush meadows and woodlands of the Fordham Hall Estate before returning to the village.

Directions

1) TR out of the pub car park and take the FP on the R to enter the churchyard. Go through the churchyard then take the L-hand path, keeping the fence to the R. Cross the track and go SA across the field. (We found a golden swathe of sunflowers here in the summer). Go down the steps, TL onto the road briefly, then take the FP on the R. (We surprised a snake basking in the undergrowth here).

2) Follow this path, ignoring paths to R and L, then go diagonally R across the field, aiming to the R of the house and on to the lane. TL to follow the lane then, ignoring the first FP on the R, take the next one by the hall. Follow this tree-lined path through to the LHFE, cross the lane, then go through a gate into a meadow. Cross the meadow, getting a glimpse of Crepping Hall through the hedge to the R. Go through the gate and continue SA, keeping to the R of the meadow. Go through the trees, over the plank bridge, continue SA and eventually go through a kissing gate to the lane. TL onto the lane and, after the bend, take the FP on the R into a meadow.

3) Proceed alongside the small stream to the L, eventually passing a lake on the L, teeming with assorted waterfowl and some woolly bovines in the field beyond. On reaching the hedge TR to walk with the hedge on the L for a few yards before taking the stile to the road. There is a very nasty blind bend here, so do cross the road with care, then go SA on the track opposite at Broom House Farm, passing some lovely old farm buildings on the R. After the black barn take the metal gate to follow the path round to the R, then cross the river and go through another metal gate. After a few yards TR through another gate, ignoring the signs for the EW for now and passing a pillbox on the R.

4) Keeping the hedgerow to the R pass a grazing field on the R and go through another metal gate to continue SA across the pasture. Take another metal kissing gate and continue on the RHFE, then cross the field ahead, go over a ditch and head slightly diagonally L, making for the back of the house. You can glimpse the beautiful half-timbered Pope's Hall over the hedge to the L. Follow the path round to the L onto a lane, passing Holly Cottage on the L. Pass under the railway and TL onto the road. TL up Bacon's Lane, passing some very pretty cottages. After a while take the FP on the R after "Brambles". Look out for the whimsical model train track crossing the path at York House. Go through a shady path onto the RHFE, passing a turkey farm on the R. Once across the field, there's a marker post with an array of signs on it.

5) This is where our section of the EW starts. At this point, if you wish to join up exactly where Walk 13 ended, you can continue along the path ahead for around 50yds to the end of the farm fence, then return to this point. Alternatively, start the EW section here. TL into the field, keeping to the LHFE. On reaching the lane, TR and go over the railway bridge, following the path round farm buildings and L through a metal gate into the field. Just before the double metal gates, which you may recognise from earlier, TR to walk alongside the river on the L.

6) What follows is a very agreeable river walk for around a quarter of a mile, keeping to the LHFE (signage is poor here). At the willow plantation, veer away from the river to continue on the LHFE for a further quarter of a mile to reach Mill Race Pillbox and continue alongside the river, passing the old railings of the garden centre on the R. We counted two swans and five cygnets nesting on the river here. Follow the path round and across a plank bridge, passing Bridge House to emerge onto the road at Ford Street. TL across the bridge and immediately cross the road to go through a gate at what used to be The Shoulder of Mutton pub.

7) Go through the trees, keeping the river on the R to reach the grounds of Fordham Hall Estate (a gift to the Woodland Trust from an anonymous donor in 2002 and eastern England's largest woodland creation site). TR at signage for Fordham Hall Estate with the river on the R. After a while veer away from the river, following the fence round to the L until reaching the road. (At the time of writing, this field was full of sheep and cows; a mixed grill, if you will. We pondered that it only needed a few pigs and we'd have the full English…). Cross the road and up the steps and TL onto a tree-lined path. After a while cross the plank bridge and continue until you reach the arched bridge over the river on the R. Just before the bridge TL **to leave the EW** and walk with the fence to the L. At the T-junction of paths TR and then L to continue uphill until reaching the lane where you TL to walk all the way back to the pub.

Bridge near Bacons Farm

The Gainsborough Line

Turners

THE ESSEX WAY IN CIRCULAR WALKS

15: Fordham to Great Horkesley

Total distance: **7.5** miles

Of which Essex Way: **4** miles

Map: OS Explorer 184 (TL 980 290)

Parking: The walk starts in Great Horkesley at the junction of Grange Road and Grantham Road, CO6 4HR where, with consideration, you can park along the street.

Pubs on route: None alas, although The Half Butt Inn, Nayland Road, CO6 4ET is just 5 minutes from the start (or, perhaps more advisedly, the end) of the walk.

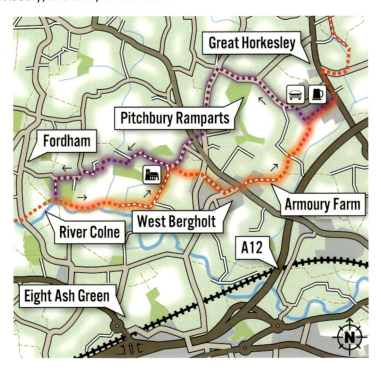

Walk Overview

The walk starts at the outskirts of Great Horkesley, with some road walking, as footpaths are limited here. We then head across farmland at West Bergholt and through ancient woodland. Then it's a peaceful walk beside the River Colne and through apple orchards back to Great Horkesley.

Directions

1) At the far end of Grange Road, take the FP through to the lane, then TR onto a short section of the EW. Walk to the end of the lane, passing the house and converted barn on the L and the orchard on the R. On reaching the fence, leave the EW to take the FP on the R. Follow this path round and TL onto the road. Follow this road for around a mile then, at the crossroads, TL to walk towards West Bergholt and Colchester. Although there is no pavement here, there are sections where you can walk along the grass verge, although you'll need to watch out for a number of drainage ditches. Stay on this road for a mile, then take the FP over a stile on the R opposite Gorse Cottage.

2) On reaching the road, cross over and go up Hall Road. At the junction at Miltor House, continue SA. TR just before the church and follow this path all the way round to the L and, just before Hillhouse Wood, take the FP on the L to head into the wood. After 20yds, at the marker post, take the R fork for a few yards then, at the noticeboard, take the R fork and eventually cross the stream to exit the wood.

3) Continue SA on the LHFE. Follow the FP round to the L and through an avenue of trees. Follow this path round to the R and TL onto the track at Kings Vineyard. Follow this path round to the R and eventually TL onto the lane. Ignore the first FP on the L and continue past the impressive Chancers House and Watercress Hall on the R. Take the next FP on the L and continue on this grassy path. Just before the wooden fence and 5-bar gate ahead, veer R and then L to walk down to the river.

4) We pick up the EW at the wooden bridge. TL over the metal-railed bridge and follow the river for a while. Eventually TL through the hedge, then immediately TR through a pasture. After a while, cross the stream, go through a metal gate and climb the track. Pass between farm buildings and TL onto the track. TL just before Cooks Cottages, ignoring the first FP on the L to take the path between fields. After a while, just before reaching the lane, follow the path L over a plank bridge to arrive opposite an impressive hall. TR, passing the church on the L, then TR to walk on the LHFE and through the gap in the hedge to follow the path round to the R. After a few yards take the L fork to head towards the houses. Follow the FP between the houses, cross the main road, then TL up New Church Road opposite.

5) Pass the church on the L and walk up to the main road. TL through the outskirts of West Bergholt. At the junction TR and, after a few yards, TL up Armoury Road. Follow this lane round to the R and, just before Armoury Farm, TL to walk along a track then SA onto the RHFE. After about 50yds, at the fingerpost, TL to walk across the field. Go over the plank bridge and then SA uphill across the next field. At the end of the next field go through the hedge on the L then TR and, after a couple of yards, take the L fork to head towards the houses. (The remains of the Iron Age hillfort of Pitchbury Ramparts is over to the L). Follow the path, keeping the orchard to the L. TR onto the lane leading up to Woodhouse Farm, then TL at the FP after Hill Side to return to the start.

Late autumn sky over West Bergholt

Chancers House

Hillhouse Wood

THE ESSEX WAY IN CIRCULAR WALKS

16: Great Horkesley to Boxted

Total distance: **8.5** miles

Of which Essex Way: **4** miles

Map: OS Explorer 184 & 196 (TL 997 332)

Parking: The walk starts at the car park at the back of St Peter's Church, Church Lane, Boxted, CO4 5TG.

Pubs on route: The Half Butt Inn, Nayland Road, Great Horkesley.

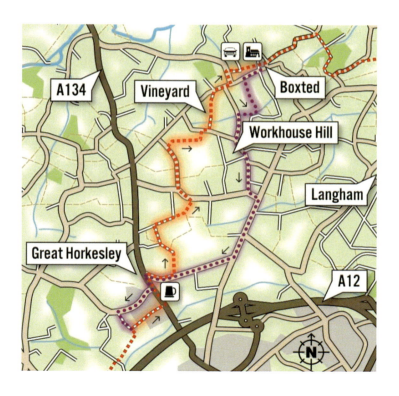

Walk Overview

An eight and a half miles that passes quickly. There is some straightforward road walking near the start to take us to the outskirts of Great Horkesley. We then follow the Essex Way through green lanes and wooded paths, and on to open countryside with attractive views of the surrounding landscape.

Directions

1) Exit the car park and TR down Church Lane, then TR onto the main road. On reaching Little Church House on the R, take the FP on the L at the metal gate and follow the LHFE. Before the gate at the end of the field TR and continue on the LHFE. TL through the trees, walk down to the lake and cross the wooden bridge, then TR. Follow this path eventually over a small plank bridge, through an avenue of trees and TL onto the lane. At the junction continue SA down Workhouse Hill for around half a mile all the way to the road, passing a cluster of pretty cottages.

2) TL onto the road for a short while, then TR to follow the main road for around half a mile, passing a garden centre on the R and eventually TR onto Horkesley Road. (We spied a lovely medley of animals through the fence on the right, including some woolly alpacas, squat guinea fowl and tufty goats). After around a mile, pass into Great Horkesley. Ignore the EW FP on the R, (we'll be picking this up on the way back). TL onto the A134 for 50yds, then TR up Coach Road. Pass the school on the R and take the FP on the L just after number 59. Follow this path eventually round to the L. (You may recognise this brief section of Essex Way from Walk 15, but for the purposes of this walk, our section of the EW starts a little further on). Walk past a large house on the R to enter a residential lane.

3) Just after Hill Side on the L, our section of the **EW picks up where Walk 15 left off.** Continue SA to the junction (where we spotted one of the old-fashioned green Essex Way signs on the Brick Kiln Lane road sign on the L). TL at the junction, passing The Half Butt Inn on the L, and Great Horkesley Manor on the R, to retrace your earlier steps for a short section along the road. TR up the next lane (Ivy Lodge Road) and take the first FP on the L just before Blackbrook Stud Farm.

4) After a pleasant tree-lined walk (during which we encountered a pair of very friendly donkeys over the fence on the R), emerge onto the lane. (Three peacocks crossed our path from one of the attractive houses here). Pass a fishing lane on the L, follow the concrete track and, as it bends to the L, TR to take track all the way to the woods. Enter the woods and pick your way through the trees, eventually veering L to go through a builder's yard, then TL onto the road.

5) After a short while take the lane on the R, ignoring all FPs until reaching Holly Lodge Cottage, then take the FP on the R, passing between farm buildings. Continue SA on this grassy track, keeping to the RHFE all the way to the woods. TL just in front of the woods, then TR onto the lane and, after a short while, take the FP on the L into the vineyard. Pass the vineyard building on the R to continue on the grassy path SA. At the end of this tree-lined path, veer slightly R and go over a small plank bridge into a field, keeping to the LHFE.

6) On reaching the lane TR, pass Wet Lane on the R and shortly afterwards take the road to the L signposted for Nayland. TR at the sign for Boxted Hall Farm. At the fork, go R and, just after Little Church House, take the grassy path to the L to walk along the LHFE, ignoring the path SA. On reaching the lane TL passing the church on the R to return to the car park.

Lake at Boxted

Thatched Cottage

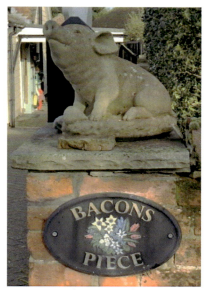
A happy piglet

Popes Cottage

THE ESSEX WAY IN CIRCULAR WALKS

17: Boxted to Stratford St Mary

Total distance: 8.5 miles

Of which Essex Way: 4 miles

Map: OS Explorer 196 (TM 043 341)

Parking: The walk starts at The Swan Inn, Lower Street, Stratford St Mary, CO7 6JR. The pub has a car park or you can park on the street.

Pubs on route: The Swan Inn, Stratford St Mary.

Walk Overview

This is a lovely walk, starting in Suffolk following the Stour Valley, then along country lanes to Boxted, where we pick up the Essex Way. We then take a scenic stroll back to Stratford St Mary with beautiful views across the Stour Valley.

Directions

1) With your back to the pub, TL down the road and, opposite Mill House, cross the road to take the FP over the river. Cross a wooden footbridge and a concrete bridge and take a metal gate to a field. Cross the field diagonally R, following signs for the Stour Valley Path and St Edmund's Way. At the end of the field, go through a metal gate and continue SA keeping the river on the R. After around 100yds, continue to follow the Stour Valley Path by turning L at the marker post and going through the hedge to TR onto a sandy path. Continue on the RHFE and follow it round to the L, then TR through the hedge and over a ditch to a path.

2) Cross over the lane that leads to Broomhouse on the R and continue SA, keeping the boundary of the house to the R. After a few yards follow the path across the field. Continue on the Stour Valley Path across the next field, making for the house ahead. Once across the field, reach a lane and leave the Stour Valley path to continue SA along the lane. Pass the art deco pumping station on the R and follow the path round to the L. After around a quarter of a mile, TR up Docuras Farm Road. On reaching the T-junction, ignore the FP SA and TL along the lane. At the junction TR and follow the road round to the R. At the next junction head toward Boxted and Colchester, passing Old Mill Road on the L. After a while TR up Sky Hall Hill.

3) At the junction just before the drive for Rivers Hall Farm, take the FP through the hedge on the L to cross the field, ignoring the EW FP to the R and eventually keeping on the RHFE, making for the houses ahead. On reaching a lane TR. At the junction TR towards Nayland to walk uphill. After a while, TR up Church Street. Then, after a few yards, take the path through the churchyard on the L and exit through the gate at the far end.

4) TR to start our section of the EW. Then TR at the end of the wall to take the alleyway back past the church. At the end of the alley, keep L onto the lane. Follow the lane for around half a mile, passing some very impressive houses and some beautiful views across the valley to the L. Take the FP to the R at Cruise Cottage onto a path through the trees and pass a lake on the R. (We saw a family of swans and cygnets here and, a bit further on, a red kite, a donkey and some unusual woolly horses in the field over to the L). A little after Potash Cottage, take the FP to the R, to circumnavigate farm buildings. Just before reaching the lane, TR to walk along the LHFE and, after a short while, ignore the first gap in the hedge and TL beside a wooden gate onto the lane. Cross the lane, SA over the grass triangle (god cake) to take the road ahead.

5) After around 200yds, take the FP on the R over a stile to go across the field, then continue SA on the LHFE. After a short while go through a gap in the hedge on the L to join a gravel track leading from a house. TR along the track. On reaching the lane, briefly TL and then take the FP on the R up the steps to cross a field. Aim for a gap in the hedge. At the marker post continue SA on the RHFE. Cross the plank bridge to continue over the next field. On reaching the lane cross over and take the lane SA. Follow the lane for around 100yds, with beautiful views across open fields to the L. Keep L at the junction and, after a few yards, take the FP to the R across the plank bridge and go slightly diagonally L, making for the gate. Once across the field cross a small plank bridge and go through a metal gate to join a grassy path.

6) At the end of the fence-line take a sharp R to walk uphill. The tower of Langham Church will soon hove into view. Follow the path round, keeping the church to the L. Just past the church, opposite the entrance to the Hall, take the tree-lined avenue to the L. Exit via the heavy iron gates at the gatehouse and TL onto the road at Gun Hill. **Take the L fork to leave the EW**, then walk through to the main road. TL passing the 16th century listed building of the exclusive Le Talbooth and cross the Stour back into Suffolk and Stratford St Mary. Follow the road back to the pub.

The River Stour

Thatched cottage

Le Talbooth

THE ESSEX WAY IN CIRCULAR WALKS

18: Stratford St Mary to Lawford

Total distance: **8** miles

Of which Essex Way: **4** miles

Map: OS Explorer 196 (TM 088 315)

Parking: The walk starts at the car park of St Mary's Church, Church Hill, Lawford, Manningtree, CO11 2JX (access via Church Hill, not the private road).

Pubs on route: The Marlborough, Mill Lane, Dedham. The Sun Inn, High Street, Dedham.

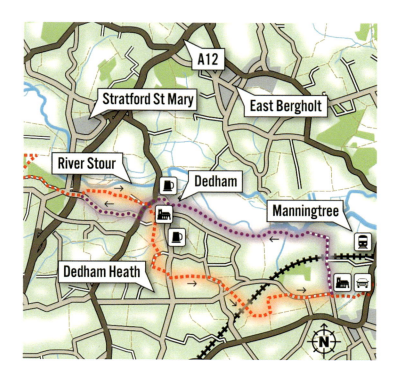

THE ESSEX WAY IN CIRCULAR WALKS

Walk Overview

Starting at Lawford, the route follows a beautiful stretch along the water meadows of the Dedham Vale, then through the village of Dedham itself, with its pretty shop fronts and tea rooms. There are some stunning views across the Stour Valley as we continue through Constable country and back to Lawford.

Directions

1) Exit the car park and go SA into the churchyard, then follow the path immediately L, keeping the church on the R, to exit the churchyard through a gate. Continue between trees to eventually emerge onto the lane by Manningtree Station. TL to follow this well-signposted path toward Flatford and Dedham. At the end of the lane TR under the railway arch and stay on this path as it winds round for around a mile, following the signs for Flatford.

2) At the National Trust Dedham Vale sign, go through the kissing gate and take the path SA signposted Dedham. After a few yards TL across a concrete bridge, through a kissing gate and TR onto the broad grassy path across the meadow. Continue SA on a concrete path, through a gate and, after a while, through another kissing gate to follow a path across the field. At the end of the field TL keeping to the RHFE. (We saw a green woodpecker climbing a tree here). Ignoring the FP on the L, continue SA to another kissing gate. Where the path ends, at the information point, go through a kissing gate and TL onto a track signposted Dedham. Keep L on the concrete track all the way to the road.

3) TR to walk along Dedham High Street, passing the Art and Craft Centre (well worth a visit) and the church on the L, and two pubs. Ignore the EW FPs to R and L (we will be using these later). Just after the three English Heritage Cottages on the L, TR up Stratford Road. (A bench has been provided along the road at a scenic viewing point across to Stratford St Mary on the R). Follow the lane all the way to Milsoms.

4) You can **begin the section of the EW** here. (If you wish to join the EW exactly where Walk 17 left off, then continue ahead across the A12 bridge for 150yds to the junction, then retrace your steps to this point). Follow the EW signage down the drive to Milsoms and, just before reaching the car park, take a sharp R through the trees. Follow the path beside the river back to Dedham. Just before reaching the road, veer L to walk beside the house and emerge onto the road. TL to walk through Dedham again.

5) Pass the church once again and, just after the war memorial, TR to pass the Duchy on the right-hand side (!). At the end of the recreation ground on the L, TR keeping to the LHFE with a view of the church to the R. After a short while TL through the kissing gates to cross the meadow all the way down to the stream. Go over a kissing gate and across a plank bride, then SA and, after a few yards, go diagonally L across a meadow to another plank bridge and through the gate. Follow the path round the buildings (noticing a perplexing memorial plaque on the wall) to exit via a metal gate onto the lane.

6) At the T-junction TR, passing some delightful cottages, then take the FP on the L at Hunter's Moon. Follow the path behind the cottage through a wooden gate and up some steps, then cross the meadow. (At the crest of the hill we could just make out the cranes of Harwich Docks ahead in the far distance, where we will be headed in our final walk). Exit the field through a wooden gate, cross the road and TR and, after a few yards, TL onto Anchor Lane and continue on the track SA, noticing some lovely views across the vale to the L. Go through a metal gate and over a plank bridge, then continue on this track through a number of gates to reach the lane.

7) TR up the lane and, after a few yards, just round the bend, take the FP to the L. Cross the field and take the kissing gate to the lane, TR and immediately L. (We found some black sheep in a garden to the R here). Pass between paddocks, cross the railway track with caution, then cross a stream to head into the woods. Pick your way through the woods and, just after the black barn, TL up the track and follow it round to the L to the next junction. Continue SA, following the path L round the bend. At the house on the L, go through the double wooden gates, then TR immediately along the RHFE to eventually reach the lane. TR and follow the lane as it bends round to the R and take the FP to the L by The Lodge. After a while look out for the FP to the R beside a metal gate which will take you back to the car park.

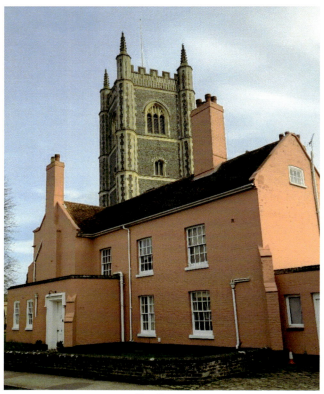

Dedham

A view across Dedham

Immaculate half-timbered cottage

THE ESSEX WAY IN CIRCULAR WALKS

19: Lawford to Mistley

Total distance: **6.5** miles

Of which Essex Way: **3** miles

Map: OS Explorer 184 & 196 (TM 121 312)

Parking: The walk starts at the car park of Mistley Village Hall, Shrublands Road, Mistley, CO11 1HS.

Pubs on route: The Red Lion, South St, Manningtree. The Crown, High Street, Manningtree.

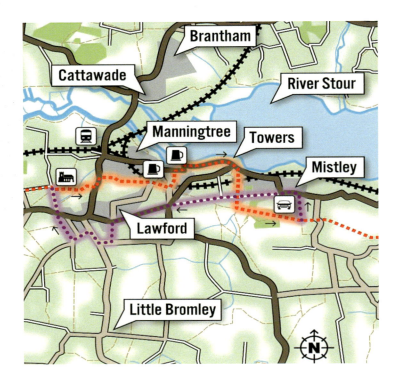

Walk Overview

We start at the village of Mistley with a pleasant amble through the wooded countryside to Lawford, before taking in the little town of Manningtree, once home to the Witchfinder General. Then it's a gentle quayside walk before returning through peaceful woods to Mistley.

Directions

1) Walk away from the Village Hall and TL at the children's playground, then keep to the R of the recreation ground. Just past the "Run and Leap" equipment, take the path to the R and, almost immediately, TL to pick your way down through the wooded area and TL onto the track (Shrubland Road). Continue on this lane for around a mile, with views of Mistley Hall across to the L.

2) At the junction go SA along Long Road, signposted Ipswich (regrettably, not the most scenic of routes, but footpaths are in short supply around here). Pass Colchester Road on the R and take the FP on the L between the houses and out onto a meadow, then TR keeping to the RHFE. On reaching the lane TR and, at the junction, exit Dead Lane and continue SA. Pass the drive to Lawford House and TL up Grange Road. Cross School Lane and, where the road bends to the L, TR through the kissing gate into the meadow. Keep to the RHFE and, after a while, go through another kissing gate into the playing field. Go SA across the field, making for the fence, and go through a small gap in the fence to the L of the black log burner chimney, to walk through to the road.

3) Cross the road to take Church Hill up towards Lawford Church. At the Rectory, **join the EW** by taking the FP on the R alongside the Old School House. Pass the church on the L and get a glimpse of estuary views ahead. Follow the FP signs downhill across the meadow, over a stream, then diagonally L across another meadow, then through a wooden kissing gate and through another meadow beside the trees, gradually walking uphill toward some cottages. Take the metal kissing gate to the lane. TL passing the cottages then, after a short while, TL onto the main road and, after a few yards, cross over to take the FP on the R at Owls' Flight Dell Conservation Area. Keep to the R, walking away from the road and, after a short while, cross a plank bridge and go uphill to follow a made-up path beside houses. Follow the path round between the pond and the backs of houses then TL onto the path beside houses, with the metal railings of the playing field on the R. Cross the road and go straight ahead up Mill Hill, passing the old waterworks building. At the end of Mill Hill TL to go over the railway bridge into Manningtree. There are a number of interesting historic buildings around here, for example the Hermitage c1580 on the R.

4) TR up South Street and follow it round passing Manningtree Methodist Church on the R and the Red Lion on the L. Pass the Manningtree Ox and, later, The Crown for a fair walk along the estuary on the L. Just before Mistley Towers, (all that remain of the 18th century Mistley Church) take the FP to the L through the trees. After a seemingly pointless circumnavigation, emerge back onto the road and TL to continue past The Mistley Thorn Hotel. (Notice the information board on the side of the hotel telling of the Witchfinder General who once lived in Mistley. Together with the Mistley Towers, The Swan Basin opposite is all that survives of an unsuccessful 18th century plan to turn Mistley into a fashionable spa town). TR in front of the old mill buildings to pick your way through to a gate to the stream. TR then TL up a set of steps under the railway bridge, through a kissing gate and across the field. (Beware, this can become something of a quagmire in the wet season). Go through a kissing gate to a lane.

5) Cross the lane and go through another kissing gate to head SA across the field. On reaching the fence-line TL. Go through another kissing gate at the end of the field to go SA uphill through Furze Wood, ignoring paths to L and R. Exit the woods and keep SA on the

RHFE. (At the time of writing, much house building was going on here, so it's possible the FP may be rerouted). On reaching power lines **TL to leave the EW** and follow the power lines between the houses. TR along Rigby Avenue then TL onto the main road and, beside Mistley Pound, continue SA up Shrubland Road back to the Village Hall.

Field path

Stour Estuary

Mistley Towers

THE ESSEX WAY IN CIRCULAR WALKS

20: Mistley to Wrabness

Total distance: 8 miles

Of which Essex Way: 3.5 miles

Map: OS Explorer 184 (TM 170 316)

Parking: The walk starts at the car park at Oakfield Wood, Wheatsheaf Road, Wrabness, Manningtree, CO11 2TF.

Pubs on route: The Village Maid, Heath Rd, Bradfield, Manningtree.

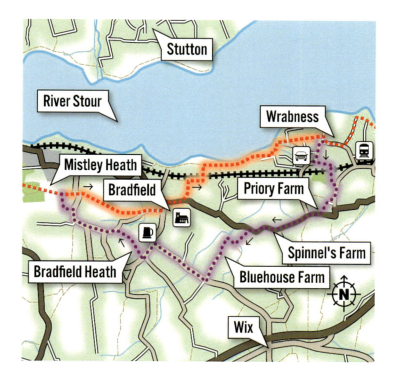

Walk Overview

Starting on the quiet outskirts of Wrabness, we take a cross-country route through farmland and woodland to Bradfield Heath and then on to Mistley Heath, taking in some stunning views across the Stour. We return via Bradfield, with a stroll beside the estuary and through a peaceful nature reserve.

Directions

1) TR out of the car park and walk down the lane. After a few yards, on the bend, TL to take the FP into the field, keeping to the LHFE. Follow the path as it bends to the L to eventually go through a metal kissing gate and go up steps to cross the railway tracks, then down the steps the other side. Go through the woods and leave via another metal kissing gate to a tree-lined path.

2) Go through the woods, over a plank bridge and TR onto the lane. Just after Domine Farm Barn on the L, take the FP on the R to cross the field, making for the houses ahead. Take the path through the L of the houses to a gravel track. Cross the track and pass in front of Foxes Farm on the R. Go through the trees then through two consecutive wooden gates. (We passed some brown sheep and woolly alpacas on the L here). Continue SA, picking your way through assorted free-range fowl, and exit via two wooden gates to the road.

3) TR and pass Priory Farm on the R, with its cunningly-fashioned sheep letterbox, for a fair walk along the road with some great estuary views. Eventually pass a lane on the L and keep to the R. (Opposite Spinnels Farm check out the stunning views of the Royal Hospital School, a public school with naval traditions, in the distance across the estuary). Where the road bends to the R, take the FP to the L beside a metal 5-bar gate. Head diagonally R across the field, heading downhill towards a tall mast on the horizon directly ahead. On reaching the treeline TL to follow the path, keeping to the RHFE uphill toward farm buildings. Pass Bluehouse Farm on the L and take the track SA. On reaching the road TR.

4) Ignore the FP to Dairy House Farm on the L and, after a fair while, take the 1st turning on the L, passing the Village Maid pub on the R and continuing L up Heath Road to the outskirts of Bradfield. Just past the Methodist Church on the R, pass Dairy House Lane and take the FP on the R between houses, go through a metal kissing gate and go SA on the path between horsey paddocks. Exit through a metal kissing gate onto a field then TR along the RHFE. At the end of the treeline, TL to walk between the fields heading towards buildings to emerge across a plank bridge to a lane, then TL to go through Bradfield Heath.

5) At the junction, continue SA and, at the next junction, keep SA at White House, then follow this road round to the R, past Dove House Farm on the L and, after 30yds, at what was once the Blacksmiths Arms at Mistley Heath, cross the green on the L and take the FP into the field, keeping to the LHFE. (There's a lot of house building going on here at the time of writing, so watch out for any rerouted FPs). After around 50yds, follow the path to the R and, at the hedge-line, **TR to join the EW**.

6) Go through a metal farm gate and merge onto a track, then TR onto the main road and, after a few yards, take the FP on the L. Go through a metal kissing gate and across a paddock then out through another metal kissing gate and through to another field. Take the broad path across the field SA, with more views of the estuary to the L and a glimpse of the cranes of Harwich docks in the far distance. Go through to the next field, across a plank bridge, and through a gap in the hedge, then across the next two fields and finally through a gate to a lane. TL up the lane to enter Bradfield.

7) TL at the junction, pass the GR post-box on the L and St Laurence Church on the R, then TR up Harwich Road, passing the charming

Milestone Cottage on the corner. (As you pass the church gates on the R, notice the gridiron motif on the gate, signifying the method of St Laurence's grisly martyrdom). Pass the impressive Bradfield Lodge on the R and a view of the estuary peeping through the houses on the L. Just past the bend take the FP to the L through a wooden gate and across fields to head down to the estuary. Halfway across the field TL and, at the railway tracks, TR. TL under the railway bridge and head SA across the field to the estuary. TR along the LHFE for a bracing walk following the estuary.

8) After a while TR into Wrabness Nature Reserve and follow the made-up path round to the L. Eventually, the EW signs will direct you off to the L and down two sets of steps to a gravel track. Take the 2nd FP on the L. Follow this path to the R across a broad plank bridge, up some steps and TR to walk along the estuary path. Go down a set of concrete steps to the R and then TL onto a path through the woods. Cross a concrete track and go SA into another covered path, beside the woodland burial ground. At the end of the path TR onto the concrete track then go over a stile to the road. **TR to leave the EW** and return to the car park.

Cottage near Bradfield

THE ESSEX WAY IN CIRCULAR WALKS

View across the Stour Estuary

Under the railway at Bradfield

21: Wrabness to Ramsey

Total distance: **6.5** miles

Of which Essex Way: **3.5** miles

Map: OS Explorer 184 (TM 211 304)

Parking: The walk starts at The Castle Inn, The Street, Ramsey, CO12 5HH.

Pubs on route: The Castle Inn, The Street, Ramsey.

Walk Overview

Starting at the little village of Ramsey, with its unassuming Grade II listed windmill, we head cross-country and through woods to Wrabness. We get a glimpse of an eccentric Grayson Perry construction, take in the unusual bell cage at Wrabness Church and stroll beside the estuary and through a peaceful nature reserve before returning to Ramsey.

Directions

1) With your back to the pub, TR to walk along the road, passing a number of interestingly-named cottages on both sides After 50yds, take the FP on the R (we're following a brief leg of the EW to start with), passing an old chapel on the L. Follow the path around the paddocks and through a wooden kissing gate, where we were taken by surprise by the windmill peering over the fence to the L. Walk diagonally across the paddock towards some kissing gates, with a cracking view of Harwich docks over to the R and a view of the church tower peeping through the trees behind. Go through the gates and diagonally R across the field, through a metal half gate, then take the FP diagonally L across the field. Go through a metal kissing gate at the corner of the field on the L and keep on the RHFE then, after a brief walk, leave the EW by going SA through a wooden gate, then keeping to the RHFE and through another metal kissing gate.

2) Take five paces straight ahead then, ignoring the path immediately to the L, TL to walk downhill. At the bottom of the hill there is a small stream on the L with a crossroads of paths and a marker post. TL across the stream and then TR, keeping the stream on the R. (Beyond this point, the signage is woefully poor, so you'll need to keep your wits about you). After around 50yds TL head for a large tree on the crest of the hill and keep to the LHFE, with a drainage ditch to the L. Keeping a row of mainly oaks to the L, follow the tree line round to the L continuing on the LHFE, with the A120 running across in front of you in the distance. At the corner of the field, at the twin-trunked oak tree, TR to walk uphill on a grassy path between fields.

3) Once across the field, cross a track and continue SA at a marker post and continue on the RHFE. At the next marker post go SA into the next field, keeping to the RHFE. At the next marker post TR at the tree line, keeping to the RHFE. Take the precarious-looking plank bridge on the R and then TL keeping to the LHFE. At the field corner continue SA through the hedge over a plank bridge to the road. TR and, after a few yards, take the FP on the L into Stour Wood. Follow the well signposted path round to the L through the woods, ignoring any junctions until the path splits at a junction marked for the car park. Take the L fork marked for the car park, ignoring the R to the hides. Cross two brief sections of rafted path and eventually exit the woods onto a track in front of Woodcutters.

4) TR to walk along the lane for a few yards then TL, (where we were enchanted by a stunning display of bluebells in the spring). Exit the woods via a metal kissing gate and continue SA on the path across the meadow with a glimpse of the estuary to the R. Pass the beautifully kept gardens of Glebe House to emerge onto a track with a railway bridge on the R. Here we have our first view of the excellent Grayson Perry's "A House for Essex", designed in the tradition of wayside chapels, as a shrine to composite Essex girl, Julie Cope. However here we TL and, on reaching the road, TR.

5) Follow this road eventually round to the R and TL in front of the station. Walk parallel with the railway on the R and the estuary beyond. TR across the railway bridge, passing The Old School on the L. There are a couple of benches along this stretch which make a lovely picnic spot, with another marvellous view of the Grayson Perry folly and the docks beyond. From here you can walk a few more yards down to the church on the R, to inspect the curious wooden bell cage. (The bell-tower collapsed in the 17th century and the bell was moved to the churchyard. However, the bell you see now is not the original and was made in 1854 by the same foundry as the Big Ben bell). If you wish to join up with exactly where Walk 20 left the EW, continue for a further 100yds beyond the church to the FP on the R just before Shrublands.

6) Retrace your steps, back past the church and **start our section of the EW** by taking the track labelled Stone Lane Caravan Site to walk down to the estuary. At the bottom of the track, on reaching the Caravan Site, TR to walk along the LHFE. Pass Shore Farm, continue along the estuary and eventually you may spot the golden roof of the Grayson Perry House glinting through the trees across to the R. (If you want a closer look at the house, it's a short walk along the next FP on the R. Or, to continue, cross a plank bridge into the woods.

7) Eventually go through a tall metal kissing gate, across a plank bridge, pass the back gardens of a beautiful house, then exit through another tall metal kissing gate and over another plank bridge. After a while, take another plank bridge and climb some steps to enter Copperas Woods nature reserve, (an ancient sweet chestnut and hornbeam coppice, designated a site of special scientific interest). Keep L following the EW signage and walking parallel with the estuary. After a while, cross another plank bridge. The path eventually wends away from the estuary uphill to the R. Exit the woods beside the wooden gate and TR to cross the railway bridge, continuing SA on the shady path between trees to eventually reach the road. TL and, after a while, opposite Copperas Wood Cottage, take the FP to the R to keep to the LHFE.

8) Go SA through the next field, with a view of the windmill across to the L, aiming for a gate in the hedgerow ahead, where we begin to retrace our steps from earlier. Go through the gate and TL, then through another metal kissing gate, then diagonally R across the field toward the windmill, through a metal half-gate. Then go diagonally L across the field, through further gates then diagonally L across the next field and through another wooden gate, following this path all the way back to the road. TL to return to the start.

Ramsey Windmill

A view of Grayson Perry's House for Essex

All Saints Church bell cage, Wrabness

A view across the Stour

THE ESSEX WAY IN CIRCULAR WALKS

22: Ramsey to Dovercourt

Total distance: **6** miles

Of which Essex Way: **3** miles

Map: OS Explorer 184 (TM 233 302)

Parking: The walk starts at the junction of Gravel Hill Way and Low Road, CO12 4UN.

Pubs on route: The Castle Inn, The Street, Ramsey.

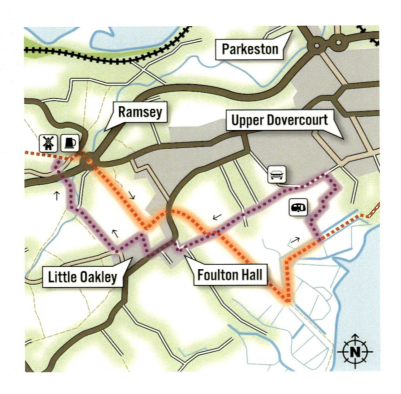

Walk Overview

From the outskirts of Little Oakley, we make our way cross-country to the small village of Ramsey. We then head down to the estuary, taking in some panoramic views, for a bracing walk along the sea wall at Dovercourt.

Directions

1) Exit Gravel Hill Way and TL onto the main road. Cross the road at the islands and continue SA. Just after the road bends to the L take the FP on the R and keep to the RHFE. Continue on a broad track, ignoring any paths to R and L for around a mile to emerge onto the road at Foulton Hall and the outskirts of Little Oakley. TL along the road for a while, passing Seaview Avenue on the L and eventually take the FP on the R at a wide gap between houses. Follow the path to the end of the houses and TL. Cross the road and continue SA to Oak Ridge, then TR to take the FP into a field, with a view of Ramsey Windmill ahead.

2) Cross the field, eventually heading downhill, then go through the trees and TR onto the path for a few yards then take the FP SA beside a derelict chimney wall, over a bridge and a stile. Go SA to the RH field corner, over a stile and SA with the hedge on the L, making for a stile in the middle of the hedgerow. Cross this rickety plank-bridge-stile combo into the next field. Go slightly diagonally L to another rickety stile, then out onto the road. Cross the road with caution to the FP ahead and go over a plank bridge into Ramsey. TR onto the lane, **where we start our section of EW.**

3) Further along the lane, pass The Castle on the L. TR and then, at the roundabout, keep to the L and cross the main road. Follow the path round to the R and L up Church Hill. Pass Ramsey War Memorial Hall on the L cross the road and pass the JW building on the R, then take the FP on the R at Windmill View. Cross a plank bridge and TL between the backs of houses and paddocks. Eventually cross another plank bridge and head across the field. Part way across the field TL at the marker post. Pass the football club, then cross the road to take the bridleway. Follow the path round to the R, keeping to the LHFE, with good views all round. (In the distance ahead, you may be able to make out the Naze Tower at Walton). At the field corner follow the path round to the L and, after around 50yds, take the steps down to the R and continue on the RHFE.

4) Keep going all the way to a final brief climb to the sea wall and TL, then through a metal gate. Follow the sea wall, dodging any grazing sheep. Eventually go through a metal gate and later, at a marker post, **go down the bank to leave the EW.** Follow the path eventually round to the R beside the chalet and caravan park. TL along the road to return to the start.

A view from the sea wall at Dovercourt

A view across Ramsey

Cottages at Ramsey

THE ESSEX WAY IN CIRCULAR WALKS

23: Dovercourt to Harwich

Total distance: **6** miles

Of which Essex Way: **3** miles

Map: OS Explorer 184 (TM 255 317)

Parking: The walk starts at Dovercourt Railway Station, CO12 3AG. There is a paying car park, or you can park in the surrounding streets with consideration.

Pubs on route: None alas.

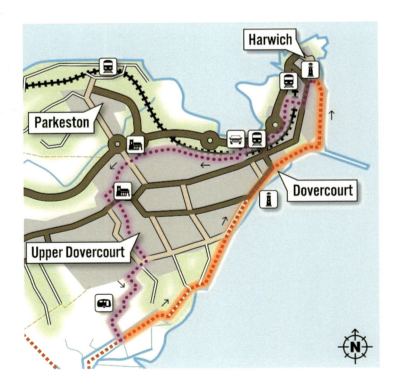

Walk Overview

If you've followed these walks in order, here we are at the final leg. Starting at Dovercourt, we make our way along shady paths to the sea front, for a bracing stretch along the sea wall at Dovercourt to the promenade at Harwich, then on to the High Lighthouse that marks the end of the Essex Way.

Directions

1) Take the FP (Station Lane) at the far end of the car park. At Pattricks Lane, take the R fork, signposted *North Sea Cycle Route*. After around a mile TR in front of The Gatehouse, pass the church lychgate on the R, then follow the path round to the L. Cross the road and take the path SA parallel with a stream on the R and the main road on the R, then eventually along the backs of houses on the L and through a wooded area.

2) Keep L here and eventually the path opens up onto a residential green. (Our intended FP seems disused and was impassable, so we have to take a brief residential route instead). Cross the green diagonally to the cul-de-sac and go SA, then follow the road round to the L. At the top of Dockfield Avenue TR and, just past no 43a, take the FP ahead. Follow this paved path along to the L and walk beside the graveyard to exit onto the main road beside the church.

3) TL and, opposite the church, cross the road to take the FP beside the school. Continue SA along Blacksmiths Lane and at the end of the road continue SA on the shady FP beside a fence on the L. After a while cross the road and continue ahead onto the next FP passing the railings of the school playing field. Eventually TR along the main road. Pass New Hall on the L and, just past Keynes Way on the R, cross the road to take the FP SA and go alongside the caravan park. Exit onto a path between fields, follow the path round to the L towards the sea wall then climb the sea wall to **start our section of EW**.

4) What now follows is a fair stretch along the coast. Continue along the sea wall, with the sandy Dovercourt beach on the R, ignoring any paths down to the beach. Pass the beach huts and continue along the promenade passing the two restored lighthouses, dating from 1863. Eventually pass the Maritime Museum (another erstwhile lighthouse) and, after 50yds, TL beside the ancient Treadwheel Crane, built in 1667, to the road. Go SA along a gravel track beside houses on the R. TR onto Old London Road to make for the High Lighthouse that marks **the end of the EW**.

5) Proceed SA to the road and TL passing Harwich Station on the R. After a while cross the road and TR down Ferndale Road. TL onto Fernlea Road, cross the next road and continue on Fernlea Road then merge onto Grafton Road. At the corner of Grafton Road take the path to the R then TL to return to Dovercourt Station.

Dovercourt lighthouses

Harwich

The High Lighthouse, Harwich

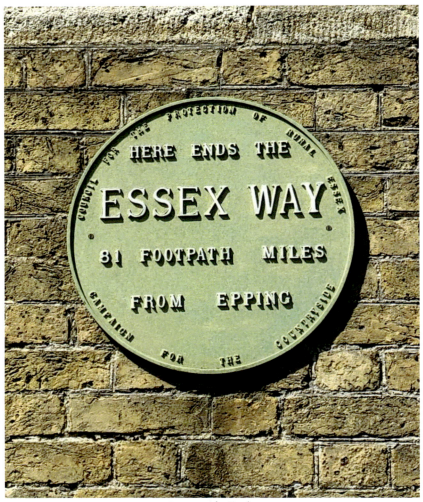
Journey's End

Further reading

Farrants, J and Bentley, P (2018) *Puddingstone Walks in Essex.* Half Way Publishing: Essex.

Gridley, D. (2010) *Walking the Lost Railways of Essex.* Slowcoach Publishing: Essex.